A Day at a Time

A Day at a Time

Thoughts and Reflections through the Seasons

Mary Kenny

NEW ISLAND

A DAY AT A TIME
First published in 2016 by
New Island Books
16 Priory Office Park
Stillorgan
County Dublin
Republic of Ireland

www.newisland.ie

PRINT ISBN: 978-1-84840-537-0
ePUB ISBN: 978-1-84840-538-7
MOBI ISBN: 978-1-84840-539-4

British Library Cataloguing Data.

A CIP catalogue record for this book is available from the British Library.

Typeset by JVR Creative India
Cover design by Karen Vaughan
Printed by TJ International Ltd, Padstow, Cornwall

10 9 8 7 6 5 4 3 2 1

In memory of my darling brothers and sister: Carlos, James and Ursula, so kind, witty, sweet-natured – if sometimes argumentative – and interested in everything. Their memory is with me every day of my life.

Contents

Summer

Autumn

Winter

Spring

Pippa's Song

Robert Browning (1812–1889)

The year's at the spring,
The day's at the morn;
Morning's at seven;
The hill-side's dew-pearled;
The lark's on the wing;
The snail's on the thorn:
God's in His heaven –
All's right with the world!

In thirty-seven words Robert Browning conjures up that rapturous feeling that we get from time to time – perhaps quite rarely, but wonderful when it occurs – that everything is in place and things are going to be just fine.

Browning, who of course married the poet Elizabeth Barrett, rescuing her from a tyrannical father and taking her off to Italy, was a dazzling Victorian poet, whose long descriptive verse 'How They Brought the Good News from Ghent to Aix' was a favourite parlour recitation in the days when people gave recitations. His 'Home Thoughts from Abroad' is the quintessence of the exile's yearning, and 'Pied Piper of Hamelin' has entered into fable and legend. How clever that he could write both at great length and with striking brevity.

St Brigid's Day

1 February

Visitors to Ireland will observe many examples of the St Brigid's cross – that rather unusual variation of a conventional cross, fashioned out of straw.

Despite a decline in formal religious practice, the St Brigid's cross retains its revered place in Irish life. Brigid lived a long time ago – she was born in the year 450 – but her memory has been stamped into Irish history and folklore. The placenames of Ireland honour her: Kilbride, Templebreedy, Toberbride, Kilbreedy, Rathbride, Drumbride. Kildare is still Brigid's county, though Alice Curtayne, in her 1955 biography of the saint, notes that there has always been special devotion to her in Offaly where Brigid established her first order of nuns at Croghan Hill, a site of the earliest Celtic monasticism.

Brigid was born into what would then have been called a mixed marriage: her father was one Dubthach (the modern equivalent is Duffy), who was a 'pagan petty king, or chieftain'. Her mother was a bondwoman, that is, a slave, by the name of Brocessa, 'who belonged to his household'. Dubthach seemed to have availed of his *droit de seigneur* and duly got Brocessa pregnant.

Ireland in 450 was on the cusp of transitioning from paganism to Christianity, in the wake of Patrick's conversions. Women had a surprising array of rights under Brehon law, but these rights were class-based. They applied to women of the chieftain class only. Slaves, or bondwomen, were without rights at all and were even forbidden converting to Christianity, since that might prove inconvenient to their masters.

Brigid, therefore, grew up with a mixed heritage, although, according to Alice Curtayne, the saint's childhood was happy – even if Ireland at this time was perpetually in a war-like state. According to the annals, between 452 and 517, fifteen major battles took place. There was a constant struggle for dominance under the rule of the High King.

When she was a teenager, Brigid's father sold her into fosterage to another chieftain (a not uncommon practice at the time). But while awaiting in her pa's chariot, she gave away his sword, complete with embedded gem, to a leper asking for alms. Lepers in Ireland, unlike the biblical kind, were not treated as outcasts. Celtic Ireland, fierce in some ways, was compassionate to the afflicted.

And so began Brigid's life of independence and defiance. She rejected marriage – Dubthach hoped she might wed a poet, but she wasn't having it – and began travelling around the country to assemble a community of women. She had seven companions with her when she was received into religious life, and by the time she died she had some fourteen thousand. She rescued women from 'the fortresses of chieftains and the hovels of bondwomen, offering them a haven'. Among her early achievements was to obtain liberty for her mother.

Eventually, recognising her evangelising ability, the bishops of Ireland extended their friendship to Brigid, and this 'developed into a kind of fellowship with the episcopacy' – that is, she was accepted as an honorary bishop herself (which was sometimes a courtesy title for abbots in those days).

Brigid was a powerful abbess and an initiator of women's communities. The annals describe her as strong, compassionate and gay (in the old sense of the word), 'imbued with a shining charity'. She was also opposed to war – she went on to confiscate many a sword.

The Danish Vikings destroyed many artefacts associated with Brigid, but the straw cross – which she wove from floor straw while comforting a dying man – lived on and remains ubiquitously with us as a reminder of a great woman.

Freedom of Choice

Every day, almost, I mentally argue with Jean-Paul Sartre and Simone de Beauvoir, the French philosopher icons of my youth. (I can hardly believe I was actually in Montparnasse, and in the vicinity of those very existential cafes where they smoked and drank coffee, at the very time they were still flourishing. But what did I know at eighteen? Nothing!)

Sartre and de Beauvoir were, and remain, the great apostles of personal freedom. Indeed, many of the accepted values of our world today were planted by the duo, first among the intelligentsia and, subsequently, taken up by the mainstream. Simone and Jean-Paul started this affirmation that everything is our own choice. Well, they didn't exactly start it: they drew on philosophical ideas already laid down, including Christian ideas of free will. Orthodox Christian theology taught that Adam and Eve were quite free to choose; they made a bad choice and paid the price. Sartrean existentialism emphasises greatly this freedom that we have – to make our choices and to accept the consequences; except, of course, their values are atheistic rather than biblical.

I argue, constantly, all the same. I aspire, most ardently, to freedom. Between freedom or equality (two values often cited as being in opposition to one another), I would always choose freedom. That's because I have sometimes experienced freedom, but I have never experienced equality – everyone I've ever met is either superior to me in one way or less fortunate than me in another (money, brains, charm, looks, skills, etc., etc.)

Yet freedom, for all that it is desired, has its elusive side too. How free are we truly? Are we subject, in our free will, to our genes, our background, our timing, our luck? Can we be free to make choices when we have duties, responsibilities and an obligation to care for others? Can we be free if we are constantly worried about money, housing, daily necessities, bills? Do we not make choices from reluctant need rather than from free will?

Sartre and de Beauvoir were childless by choice, and that was an element in their freedom. But was it also an element in their lack of insight into the everyday lives of the rest of us? I go on debating with their shadows.

The Ethics of Prostitution?

A man asked my advice about whether he should visit a prostitute. He was a widower in his eighties and he missed his wife – and their sex life. He didn't want another 'involvement' in a relationship: he just wanted some sexual companionship. Well, I said, taking the coward's way out, it's up to yourself and your conscience. I have interviewed women who worked as prostitutes – 'sex-workers' is now the accepted term – over the course of my journalistic career and what struck me about them was their contempt of men. I've interviewed men who have frequented prostitutes and they have joked (men often joke about things that disturb them) that hookers and psychiatrists are the only two professionals who insist on cash as the transaction is done – because the service provider would never get the money once the encounter is in the past.

Yet there are people who speak kindly of women who sell sex. My brother Carlos was touched by the stories he had heard in France during the 1940s about the women who provided sexual services to *les gueles cassées*. These were war veterans whose faces had been disfigured and were considered to be repellent to women in the normal course of events. But certain prostitutes overcame such repulsion and provided sexual services for these veterans (cheerfully, he alleged). Perhaps this is an example of where money can buy a form of compassion.

The French had a more practical approach to sex-work (although in modern times their attitudes are changing, perhaps under pressure from feminism). Gaston Berleymont was for many years the landlord of The French pub in Soho – his parents had founded it in the 1920s, and during the Second World War the Free French, including de Gaulle, had met and sipped there. In his retirement days, Gaston spoke nostalgically about the French prostitutes who had frequented Soho after the war. 'They had such beautiful manners. Never plied for trade in the pub. And they never missed Mass on Sunday at St Patrick's church' – the very pretty Catholic church in Soho Square. But, I asked him, was there not a contradiction between their lifestyle and religious devotions? 'Why should there be?' he asked. 'Their profession had nothing to do with their faith.' It was suggested to me subsequently that their faith may have helped them bear their profession. Keeping body and soul together drives most of us to work: sometimes the problem is trying to keep them apart.

When Doctors Err

It's often said that we learn more from our mistakes than we do from our successes. But imagine being a surgeon, making a mistake with an operation and having to sit through a revision while you 'learn' from what went wrong – perhaps knowing that someone died because of your error. The brain surgeon Henry Marsh describes this process very poignantly in his book, *Do No Harm* (the ancient Greek Hippocratic oath, for doctors, begins: 'First, do no harm.') He actually delivered a lecture in America with the title 'All My Worst Mistakes': I'm not sure that many of us would have the courage to stand up in public and make such an avowal.

'Everybody accepts that we all make mistakes,' he writes, 'and that we learn from them. The problem is that when doctors such as myself make mistakes the consequences can be catastrophic for our patients.' Most surgeons, he says, with a few exceptions, feel a deep sense of shame when their patients suffer or die as a result of their efforts, 'a sense of shame which is made all the worse if litigation follows'. Doctors, he confesses, find it difficult to admit to making mistakes, to themselves as well as to others, and there are all kinds of ways that they can disguise these errors or put the blame elsewhere.

It was only when approaching the end of his career that Marsh felt an increasing need to 'bear witness' to his past mistakes. This was in the hope that anyone following in his footsteps might learn from the blunders, and also, perhaps, as a kind of reckoning with his life's work. Then, 'the more I thought about the past, the more mistakes rose to the surface, like poisonous methane stirred up from a stagnant pond. Many had been submerged for years.'

When he delivered his American lecture, it was met by stunned silence. He still wonders if his audience was astonished by his reckless honesty or by his incompetence.

Yes, a brain surgeon can indeed make a mistake. Cutting through an artery when operating, with fatal results, is an acknowledged hazard of brain surgery. It is a devastating loss to a family, especially when the patient is young and had a good chance of recovery.

Who would be a brain surgeon?

World Cancer Day

4 February

I've had this pain – or is it an ache? – between my shoulder blades for about, oh, let's see, five or six months now. I don't feel otherwise unwell and, mostly, I just hoped it would go away. Sometimes it does go away. But then it comes back. And there is always this awful calculation in your head: if it is a fatal cancer tumour, wouldn't it better, really, not to know about it? On the other hand, if it is something treatable, isn't it sensible and responsible to have it checked out?

I had a distant aunt who had a bad shoulder for a while. Her GP had described it as 'frozen shoulder', which is something muscular, as I understand. Eventually, the condition warranted further investigation. Further investigation put her in a hospice for the dying – it was bone cancer – and she departed this world quite speedily.

Maybe she was better thinking it was a frozen shoulder, the previous year, when she still enjoyed life. 'In greater knowledge is greater sorrow,' says the Book of Ecclesiastes.

Cancer is the diagnosis we all fear so much, and it is also the diagnosis that many of us will one day face, should we live long enough. An oncologist describes it as essentially a disease of old age, even though it can strike at the young, tragically. We have all seen the ravages that cancer has wrought: my brother James died of a cancer that originally started in the kidney, at the age of fifty-two, and my sister Ursula died of a gynaecological cancer at the age of sixty-nine. I dreaded seeing the cancer look that makes the face, and the body shape, so skeletal.

And yet, I know many friends who have survived cancer: cancer of the breast, cancer of the prostate, cancer of the bowel. I know a woman who has survived cancer three times. So much progress has been made, and so many people are incalculably brave in facing treatment and prognosis.

When I was growing up, the word 'cancer' was only mentioned in hushed tones. In some London newspapers, journalists were not permitted to write the word itself, lest it bring 'bad luck'. On World Cancer Day, let's thank the medical researchers who have worked so hard to cure this frightening illness and have made so much progress.

The Uses of Superstition

Every time I see a lone magpie, I think of my late brother Carlos. Glimpsing the bird alone, he would wait and wait and wait until a second bird joined the first, bearing in mind the old superstition: 'One for sorrow, two for joy.' One lone magpie is deemed to be bad luck.

These are folklore traditions which don't have any basis in rationality, and I tell that to myself when the lone magpie alights upon my path. The bad luck that the lone magpie may bring can, according to superstitious protocol, be deflected by greeting the magpie with the words: 'Good morning, Mr Magpie. And how is your lady wife today?' Most birds mate for life, and thus it is that the lone bird is, perhaps, himself unlucky.

Superstitions have a bad influence on human behaviour where they replace rational thinking; where they cause people to be passive and fatalistic, rather than exercising their free will; and where they act as self-fulfilling prophesies. If you think something will bring bad luck, perhaps your unconscious will court bad luck.

My brother was a very intelligent man and a well-read person; I ponder on his predilection for superstitions and wonder about their origin. He was tended, as a young boy, by a Dublin woman my mother engaged as a housekeeper, Lizzie, and Lizzie had many superstitious ideas, often mixed in with Christianity. Dubliners of that generation also had a morbid streak: when Carlos was a young boy, Lizzie would take him to see drowned sailors stretched out in the mortuary in Ringsend – it was, it seems, quite a spectacle back in the 1930s. Some of these poor fellows made 'a lovely corpse', in Lizzie's words.

But there is also a wise element within superstitions. They may remind us that our lives are contingent. We do have choices, but we don't always have control over nature or happenstance, and bad luck can strike out of the blue. The magpie may not bring me bad luck, but he may remind me that 'stuff happens' to people, out of nowhere. So don't go about your day feeling cocky that you've got everything beautifully under control.

The magpie's bad reputation, according to Chloe Rhodes in her book *One for Sorrow*, may stem from its behaviour: it's known for stealing shiny objects and for killing other birds' chicks. Or perhaps it is that in good weather magpies tend to be in groups – in foul weather, alone.

The rhyme that begins with 'one for sorrow' and ends with 'six for gold / Seven for a secret never to be told', somehow connects us to centuries of country lore.

A Carer's Lot

Whenever I encounter someone who has been thrust into the position of being a carer – be it a son or daughter for an elderly parent or a spouse for a long-term partner now diagnosed with a degenerative condition – my advice is always this: make time for yourself. Give yourself breaks. Get respite care.

When I was the main carer for my late husband, a friend gave me this advice – and a good illustration of why it's important. You know when you're in an aircraft and the flight attendants start demonstrating the safety drill? They always add that, in case of an emergency, you must put on your own oxygen mask before you help anyone else, including a child.

That's because unless you equip yourself with the wherewithal you won't be in a position to help anyone else. A useful metaphor.

Carers are often dogged by a sense of duty and a sense of guilt (as well as genuine feelings of love and wanting to care for someone). They can feel isolated, imprisoned and depressed by their role of caring – even when they want to do it and would hate to desert their caree.

That's why they have to look after themselves. They have to get breaks. Respite there must be.

Someone who is stricken with a severe disability or a degenerative illness can easily feel abandoned, yes, and can even return to a child-like sense of dependency. I remember arranging to pick up my husband after a hospital appointment – at a time when he was beginning to decline in health (from a stroke) – and, because of traffic congestion on a motorway, I arrived rather later than arranged. (It was before the era of the mobile phone – not that Richard would ever have acquired, or used, a mobile phone.) He was sitting waiting for me in the hospital waiting room, and as I entered, the look on his face was like that of a rescued child. This from a man who had been the very epitome of independence, famous for vanishing from a pub in a puff of smoke and turning up in Saigon.

The carer has to make respite arrangements with a certain degree of guile, inventing some valid excuse for an absence – an excuse that won't hurt the caree or make him feel abandoned. But it must be done. As my aunty Nora used to say: 'When you're too good, you're no good.'

Lent: When Less Was More

Old customs change and die away. Ash Wednesday was an important day in my childhood because it was the beginning of Lent,
and Lent, to Catholics in the 1950s, was rather what Ramadan is
to Muslims today. It is probable that more people in the Western
world are now familiar with Ramadan than they are with Lent. For
forty days (with a crucial break for St Patrick's Day on 17 March)
we observed fasting and abstinence – no meat on Wednesdays
or Fridays, no sweets or treats and no weddings or dances either.
Grown-ups would usually forswear alcohol for the fasting period.

The season of Lent marks the forty days that Jesus spent in the
wilderness, but it also draws upon agrarian practices from when
our societies were based on agriculture: the winter stocks were
running low and the hens wouldn't start laying again until April,
so the shriving of Lent blended in with food practices and needs.

In continental Europe, Carnival and Mardi Gras preceded Lent
with parties and feastings, but Shrove Tuesday never quite had
the same cachet and was reduced, finally, to Pancake Day, the last
residue of what was once a European *kermesse*.

If there is a secular Lent now, it is likely to be in January, when
people shrive their bodies after the indulgences of the Christmas
period.

The rhythm of the year has changed: refrigeration and the deep
freeze, as well as the jet engine, have dictated the changes. There

is now no season when strawberries are not available, and food is air-freighted from all over the globe. If we really cared about the environment we would not fly vegetables in from Kenya and flowers and fruit from South America. We would eat local foods when they are in season and be content with them.

But we're spoiled by our consumerism, so we want everything at our convenience and for our delectation at all times. And so we will never quite know the joys of feasting after fasting, and the particularly exquisite taste of a rasher of bacon on a Saturday morning when it has been beyond our legitimate reach on the Friday.

The Charm of the Feline

Pussolini walked into our lives by appearing at the garden door and making it plain – as cats will do – that she would appreciate a meal. So I rushed to the corner shop and purchased some cat food, and from then on she decided to adopt us. She's a classic moggie, and she must have another – a 'real' – owner, and perhaps we should have tried to find out who that was. She did have a collar around her neck but, mysteriously, she removed it. She's a frightfully clever cat: she 'tells' you when she wants to go out and come in, when she wants food and when she simply wants to sit on your lap and purr. She also dances. If you bend down to pet her head, she rises on her hind legs and does a beautiful little Nureyev step or two.

My son named her Pussolini because cats share certain characteristics with Italian dictators: everything must be on their terms; they demand devotion to Uno Gatto; and they decide which territory shall be theirs. She's also given to sly fits of temper – stalking off if she doesn't like the food that has been put out. She once decided she didn't like fish, and that was that.

In addition to their powers of command, felines have powers of beauty. The grace of their musculature as they move is something to behold – again, one is reminded of the ballet dancer. And then they sit on your knee, sometimes curling up in guileful imitation of a baby, nestling into your lap and rewarding you with what you think are adoring looks when you caress their back.

Pusso comes and goes as she pleases. She makes it clear that it's her choice. Sometimes she disappears for a day or so, and at the end of twenty-four hours I begin to worry that something has happened to her. I'd miss her terribly if she went away permanently, and even her temporary absence is a reminder that all attachments, in the end, are severed by death. When she's absent, I look at her empty food plate a little sadly. And then, as if out of nowhere, she appears at the garden door again, and her return is greeted with the feline equivalent of the fatted calf.

'Don't Be Thin-Skinned'

Mother Margaret Mary stood in front of our class of sixteen-year-olds. A practical, dedicated nun whose rote approach to French verb endings was remarkably effective (*ais/ais/ait* ...), she liked to dispense sensible advice. 'Now, girls,' she began. 'Don't be *touchy*. Nobody likes a touchy person. A person who takes offence at the slightest provocation. A person who flies into moods, tempers and tantrums. A person who is thin-skinned and over-sensitive to every slight. If someone says something that offends you, just brush it off. Go for a walk. Forget about it. Move on. But don't be *touchy*.'

I remember this advice so well: I can see her saying it, while we sat on the orchestra steps of the concert hall. Did I follow it? Sometimes. Sometimes not. Maggie May – her colloquial name – lived before the time of research into genetic predisposition, when we would learn that many of our characteristics are inherited, and if we're 'touchy' or over-sensitive, maybe we can't help it. Touchiness was certainly in my family – and still is, at times. I had an aunt who was so super-sensitive that she saw slights everywhere and the world as a cruel place which delivered many affronts. And it was her further lifelong torment to be overweight.

She was lodging with a companion in the English midlands and one night was asked to put the milk bottles out – in the days when empty milk bottles were deposited on the doorstep for the early-morning milkman. Aunt Nora felt this was a slight – she thought it demeaned her to servant status – and departed from the shared accommodation, which was otherwise delightful, the next day.

Super-sensitivity was in her character but possibly, too, endorsed by experience. She had once been told of a fashionable Victorian nervous condition, 'neurasthenia', from which women were said to suffer. It just means being thin-skinned.

I experience mild tendencies to paranoia myself. If someone ignores me, I think they hate me, when the usual case is that people are just too busy with themselves to remember to attend to someone else. Although, being paranoid doesn't mean people *don't* loathe you.

If Maggie May lived in an era before genetic predisposition assigned us our traits, she also lived in an age before political correctness (which is not all bad) encouraged us to take offence so prodigiously. But, essentially, she was right: we should try not to be touchy.

A Blessing We Should Count

When oldies recollect their childhoods, they often remember a visit to the dentist as being akin to entering a torture chamber, with the frightful treadle drill and a nauseating smell of antiseptic. The dentist's chair has remained as an emblem of torment because of such memories. Laurence Olivier did the dental profession no favours when he portrayed the cruel and sinister Nazi dentist in *Marathon Man* applying excruciating oral pain to Dustin Hoffman. It hits a nerve – not because dentists are cruel people, but because, lying back in the dentist's chair, we feel vulnerable.

But dentists should be declared heroes, really. They have hugely advanced the health and even happiness of humanity. They have consistently relieved pain and are always developing new ways to advance dental surgery.

Dentists themselves can suffer from 'transmitted stress' – the stress felt by the patient in the dental chair is communicated to them – and until recently had quite low actuarial ages of death.

They are also said to feel 'status anxiety', because dentists traditionally don't have quite the same social position as doctors. There's no Jewish joke about the proud mother on a Florida beach shouting – 'Help, my son the dentist is drowning!'

And yet, in America, good dentistry has been greatly prized for decades. When a Balkan friend of the family – a university professor – asked if my sister could help him get a visa for America, Ursula replied: 'Yes, but he can't go to America with those teeth! The taxis would never pick him up! He'll have to see a dentist!' True, the Serbian academic had poor teeth, but until then I hadn't realised that bad teeth could be such a stigma in the US. (Question at Homeland Security: 'Are you now or have you ever been a member of the Communist Party, or do you have bad teeth?')

When the novelist Martin Amis obtained a million dollars for a book advance in the 1990s, he said he needed the money to fix his teeth. This was considered an outrageous act of vanity in London – 'All that money for a Liberace smile?' – but in New York, it was thought entirely rational.

Look at any set of American teeth and you'll usually see a perfect set of gnashers. They may be capped, polished, assisted by implants and cosmetically whitened, and thus they are faultless.

Advanced dentistry has now crossed the Atlantic, and the costs are reflected proportionately. But I think that dental care always cost money. In the 1920s and 1930s, people would have all their teeth extracted at a young age so as to save the expense – and pain – of visiting the dentist for the rest of their lives.

Some people still fear visiting the dentist – one person in ten has some phobia about getting into that chair. It's a pity because modern dentistry can do wonders and can change lives. But children today have a much more positive attitude. My granddaughters shout 'Hooray!' when they're due a trip to the dentist, because they get all kinds of stickers and colouring books as rewards. It may help that many dentists attending to young children are women, who may indeed be better at treating the very young.

Arthur MacMurrough Kavanagh, a Westminster MP for Carlow in the 1860s, was born without legs or arms, yet he wrote at the end of his life that the greatest affliction he had known was excruciating toothache. We should appreciate the great achievements of modern dentistry a lot more than perhaps we do.

The Rules for Social Kissing

What are the rules for social kissing? No one seems to know for sure. An expert in modern manners tells me that, among the gentry classes, they are: 'two in town, one in the country' (you kiss on both cheeks when in the city, on one when in your rural abode).

But I don't think this is rigidly laid down anymore. It's really all very flexible. What we *can* say is the British and the Irish kiss a great deal more than they used to do. It used to be polite to shake hands and to kiss one's nearest and dearest on significant occasions, but even then it depended on the family. I know of families – Scots, actually – who grew up avoiding all kisses and hugs. There was even a school of child psychology, prevalent in the 1930s, that to kiss children too much was to 'spoil' them. Queen Mary, the wife of King George V, and of German extraction, as it happens, thought that kissing boys would soften them up too much. Her eldest son, David, couldn't face being king without the woman he loved – the twice-divorced Mrs Simpson – so we might assume that he was lacking in kisses. Her second son, Bertie, who became George VI, was a nice man but a nervous wreck who couldn't get through his coronation without a ciggie (which makes him seem very likeable) and had a dreadful stammer.

When I was a companion to an elderly French lady – very worldly-wise – back in the 1960s, she tutored me on her social rules for kissing. Kissing in public, she explained, was a signal of peer equality: persons should kiss those who are of the same rank as themselves. For example, if the wife meets the mistress at an opera soirée and the mistress is of the same rank, they kiss. 'But if the mistress is just some little ballet dancer, the wife does not acknowledge.'

I notice that world leaders who regard each other as peers kiss when meeting. Monarchs of the same rank also exchange the public kiss: the Queen of Denmark with the Queen of the Netherlands; the Queen of the Belgians with the King of Spain. All very interesting to observe, but I'm still not entirely sure when I'm supposed to do it and when not.

Things You May Not Know about St Patrick

17 March

- Patrick was a teenage atheist. In his famous 'Confession' he actually says he was an atheist from childhood. He got religion in Ireland, while tending sheep as a slave labourer at Slemish, Co. Antrim.
- There were some Christians in Ireland prior to Patrick's arrival in 432, evangelised by Palladius. We could be celebrating St Palladius's day on 7 July.
- But most of the native Irish were pagans who worshipped a number of gods, including Dagda, Aengus and Ogma. The favourite seems to have been Lug, after whom Lughnasa – August – is named. Brian Friel's play *Dancing at Lughnasa* has a subtext of celebrating Lug at harvest time.
- Patrick was born at Bannaventa Berniae, which is somewhere on the west coast of Britain, between the Clyde and the Severn.
- Some have claimed he was born in France, but it's not probable. There was a French connection, though, because he trained for the priesthood at Auxerre, in Burgundy. He passed two years in this exquisitely gastronomical part of Gaul before returning to the misty shores of Erin.

- His mother was called Concessa. Patrick's original name was Sochet. Ultan, Bishop of Connor, also referred to Pat as 'holy Magonus'.
- He never claimed to have banished the snakes from Ireland. Neither was he historically associated with the colour green. All that branding came later.
- But he did quickly perceive that the Celts were nature-worshippers, and nature is always associated with green.
- Patrick was very attached to the Holy Trinity, which he mentions frequently in his writings, and the shamrock, surely one of the world's most successful logos, is a fine visual metaphor of the doctrine of the Trinity of Father, Son and Holy Spirit. The Trinity is mentioned in the preamble to the Irish Constitution: some secularists would like to remove it, thus losing a special connection with Ireland's founding saint.
- Irish women were early devotees of Patrick's evangelisation. Wealthy ladies laid their jewellery at his altar, but he apparently returned the gifts as he didn't relish a special association with luxury.
- St Pat said that 'a Christian must pay his debts' (according to the Harvard scholar Philip Freeman in his book, *The World of St Patrick*).
- Did Patrick speak Irish? He must have done to communicate so successfully, although Latin was the common language of Christianity at the time.
- In his first episcopal synod, he condemned the Celts' 'belief in vampires'. Bad news for Bram Stoker.
- Patrick converted the Irish quite peacefully, though there were some close calls. The High King Loiguire at Tara threatened to have Patrick slain at one point, but in a confrontation with

the Druid priests, St Pat seems to have won them over. He was supported by the High Queen.

- Paddy's Day has been marked for centuries but only became a national holiday in Ireland in 1903, thanks to British legislation ushering in bank holidays. Its growth in popularity was greatly helped by the Irish diaspora, especially in America.
- St Patrick's Day is now one of the most globally marked national days in the world: bells ring out from Buenos Aires to Shanghai, rivers are dyed green and Jewish New Yorkers eat emerald bagels for the day. It has been through many transformations, but never lost its essential cordiality and its note of benign, unthreatening national jollification.

Panic Stations

Oh, panic, panic, panic. Who doesn't know that chilling feeling in the stomach of being frightened, apprehensive, anxious and panic-stricken? You're going to the hospital for a serious medical test; you're called to the boss for a worrying one-to-one talk; you have to give someone bad, or uncertain, news; you have to make a public speech; you may have to fire someone; you may face redundancy yourself; you feel you are looking into an abyss and you don't know what to do; you're in despair about the number of bills on your desk; you don't know how you'll get through the day.

Or sometimes it can be something comparatively trivial that has you burying your face in your hands: the printer doesn't work; the car has a puncture; you missed a train.

There's an inspiring American author and teacher – now dead – called Susan Jeffers who has a very good mantra for all these crises. 'I'll handle it.' Keep saying over and over again, 'I'll handle it.' If I get a diagnosis of a serious illness: 'I'll handle it.' If I'm apprehensive about paying the bills: 'I'll handle it.' If I'm worried about my family: 'I'll handle it.' If I wake up feeling that what I have to do during the day is too much for me: 'I'll handle it.' You may not handle everything in the best way, but you'll handle it as best you can. This phrase has really helped me in difficult circumstances.

I remember being sacked on one particular occasion – most seasoned journalists have been fired at some stage (a bracing experience from which one learns much) – and thinking: 'This is catastrophic.' I saw that cheque which arrived monthly into my account dissolve before my eyes. God knows it happens to millions and I remember the exact moment: I was standing at a bus stop in New York when the call came through. I didn't know the Jeffers mantra then but, in retrospect, it worked out: I handled it.

Susan Jeffers also advises that you should tell yourself that if you don't get to do what you had banked on doing then you'll do something else. Quite so.

The name of her best-known book is *Feel the Fear and Do It Anyway*: a title which is altogether self-explanatory.

Why (Almost) No Agony Uncles?

I chaired a meeting a little while ago in which four veteran 'agony aunts' – counsellors, in magazines or newspapers, who reply to readers' problems – spoke about their accumulated experiences of answering letters and, nowadays, emails. All human life presents itself in these columns and, most particularly, that which concerns relationships, family issues, sex, marriage, anxieties and health, both mental and physical.

One of the questions from the audience was: 'Why are there no agony uncles? Why are men never chosen to address relationship problems?' There were various benign answers from the panel, amounting to the view that, while there have occasionally been men doing the job – Graham Norton is rather a good counsellor in this field – they were nonetheless rare and women are the natural dispensers of, shall we say, grandmothers' wisdom.

But I thought about an amusing email that an Irishman had sent me on this very theme, in the form of a problem letter to an imaginary agony uncle (penned before the era of the mobile phone):

Q. Dear Walter,
I hope you can help me here. The other day I set off for work, leaving my husband in the house watching TV as usual. I hadn't gone more than a mile down the road when my engine conked out and the car shuddered to a halt. I

left it by the roadside and walked back home to get my husband's help. When I got there I couldn't believe my eyes.

He was in the bedroom with a neighbouring lady – a flirtatious blonde, I might add – making mad, passionate love to her. I am thirty-two, my husband is thirty-four and we have been married for twelve years. When I confronted him, he broke down and admitted that he'd been having an affair for the past six months.

I told him to stop or I would have to leave him. He was let go from his job six months ago and he says he has been feeling increasingly depressed and worthless. I love him very much, but ever since I gave him the ultimatum he has become increasingly distant. I don't feel I can get through to him anymore. Can you please help?

Distraught of Dublin

A. Dear Distraught,

A car stalling after being driven a short distance can be caused by a variety of faults with the engine. Start by checking that there is no debris in the fuel line. If it is clear, check the jubilee clips holding the vacuum pipes onto the inland manifold. If none of these approaches solves the problem, it could be that the fuel pump itself is faulty, causing low fuel delivery pressure to the carburettor float chamber or fuel injection system.

I hope this helps solve this annoying problem.

Walter

A satire can sometimes capture a common perception (even a stereotype), and this comedic passage seeks to explain why questions about relationships are so often addressed to women – and usually addressed, too, by the traditional agony aunt.

The Pursuit of Happiness

20 March

What is happiness? Dear me – philosophers have pondered on this for centuries, ever since the Greeks first considered the question, and there have been many definitions of this blithe spirit. Richard Whately, the Archbishop of Dublin in the Victorian period, said, wittily and pithily: 'Happiness is no laughing matter.' Jane Austen told us that: 'A large income is the best recipe for happiness I heard of. It certainly may secure all the myrtle and turkey part of it.' The German philosopher Immanuel Kant warned us that: 'Happiness is not an ideal of reason, but of imagination.' The utilitarian Jeremy Bentham believed it was the business of the state to consider: 'The greatest happiness of the greatest number ... the foundation of morals and legislation.' And of course the American Declaration of Independence promises, in the words of Thomas Jefferson, that among the rights that are 'inalienable' are 'the preservation of life, and liberty, and the pursuit of happiness'.

Can happiness be pursued? Or, as the Greek philosophers, I believe, came to conclude, is it more usually a serendipitous by-product of something else: moments of epiphany when something is achieved, love is conquered, a child is born, luck comes our way? Or is it, as Alexander Pope seemed to imply, a question of disposition? Watching a rich, nervous man and a happy-go-lucky poor one, he observed that 'one flaunts in rags / One flutters in brocade'. Some modern geneticists suggest this is the case: you may be fortunate enough to draw on happy genes. You're the happy-go-lucky type. That would be apt, for the very word 'happy' comes from 'hap' meaning 'chance': 'hapless' is 'luckless'.

Or is it a mistake to expect, or even strive for, happiness? My elder son, who is something of an expert on Friedrich Nietzsche, reminds me that Nietzsche concluded that the natural lot of the human race wasn't happiness but struggle. It is struggling with life's difficulties that brings us a sense of meaning.

Still, we do surely wish for happiness: we wish each other happy birthday and happy Christmas and happy New Year and happy days ahead. Many a parent says about their child: 'I don't mind what he/she is or does, so long as he/she is happy.' Since it's a normal human aspiration, it's haply indeed that 20 March has been deemed International Day of Happiness. So go and be happy. And if you're not happy, then 'fake it till you make it'.

'You have enemies? Good. That means you've stood up for something, sometime in your life.'

Winston Churchill

Jobs of the Future

Because journalism has been changed utterly, and probably imperilled, by the advent of the Internet, I often think about the number of trades and professions which are predicted to disappear or diminish with the onward march of computers, robots and artificial intelligence.

Within the past few decades the jobs of book-keepers, cashiers and telephone operators have all but gone. Computers have replaced airline-reservation clerks and greatly reduced the services of travel agents. Estate agents are said to be doomed, as the computer software which searches and defines the property you're searching for (or selling) gets evermore sophisticated.

Robots and artificial intelligence are taking over a whole range of sales, like the automated supermarket checkout presided over by an annoying robotic voice which tells you that there is an unexpected item in the bagging area.

Which jobs or professions will last into the future for our grandchildren? The folks who set up the algorithms are already working out the predictions. It's calculated that in the United States 47 per cent of current jobs are 'at risk' of being replaced by some form of artificial intelligence.

Anything that can be done by a machine will be done by a machine. You might think that only a teacher can teach, but there are evermore online teaching programmes available, and university teaching itself has been highly computerised – one of the aspects of studying for a part-time MA that I found discouraging. The machine seemed to replace the tradition of the tutor with whom you might have a rewarding conversation. Ask a question at a seminar and you were referred to a 'download'.

Education online will make it more accessible to more people: my son taught himself Italian with the help of an online language-learning programme. But by the same token, private language tutors have noticed a decline in business because they've been replaced by an Internet service.

Teaching and assessment by computer, say the boffins, will be increasingly 'calibrated to match students' needs'. Oh yeah. The great boast of these computer boffins, too, is that artificial intelligence 'has no bias', since it has no emotions. Therefore it will be fairer.

A study was done of Israeli judges which showed that their lordships tended to hand out more lenient sentences after a decent lunch. A computer would never be liable to such human inconsistencies; and, yet, isn't there something endearing, and an element of lucky chance, perhaps, about such foibles? The accused might cherish the hope that he'll be in the dock after a spot of Cabernet Sauvignon has been partaken.

The predictions are that legal and financial services will be vulnerable to takeover by artificial intelligence. Some medical tasks, such as diagnostics, are better done by machines than people – indeed, there's a computer at the famous Memorial Sloan Kettering cancer hospital in New York which is apparently ace at this.

Anything to do with machinery is vulnerable to the eradication of human employment. All agricultural technology will be robotised, as will many agricultural tasks: robots in Spain already do some vegetable-picking. Well, harvesting fruit and veggies has always been a back-breaking job.

Two Oxford academics, Frey and Osborne, wrote a paper on the future of employment claiming that 'robots are capable of producing goods with higher quality and reliability than human labour'.

Yet even the boffins concede that not all jobs can be done by robots and artificial intelligence. We're glad to be informed that robots 'cannot yet match the depth and breadth of human perception'.

Anything that requires the human touch will still be in demand. You can't get your hair done over the Internet. You can't eat machinery – real food will always be needed. Anything that requires 'negotiation, persuasion and care' is likely to remain within the ambit of humans.

So mental-health therapists, social workers, choreographers, artists, actors and clergy seem assured of continuing employment opportunities. Administrators and supervisors in specialist areas will always be needed. Don't you sometimes just long to talk to a human being in a business encounter?

Predictions can never be exact because there is always an unexpected factor, and there's often a reaction against the machine. People will always need people.

Down Syndrome Day

21 March

That great American playwright Arthur Miller fathered a son with Down syndrome, Daniel, in 1967, born of his third marriage, to Inge Morath – famously, Miller's second wife was Marilyn Monroe, by whom (to her great sorrow), he had no children. Arthur Miller, who was born in 1915, already had two children by his first marriage. And soon after Daniel was born, he was consigned to an institution. In his compelling memoir, *Timebends*, Miller could not bring himself to include Daniel among his children and did not mention Daniel in his will either. It is sometimes said that fathers are more dismayed by having a child with a disability than mothers: for mothers, the maternal instinct may come more quickly to the rescue, and Daniel's late mother, Inge, was reluctant to institutionalise him, but she seems to have been persuaded to do so.

Arthur and Inge Miller had another child, Rebecca, and some years after her parents' death Rebecca took her brother Daniel back into her family circle and he is now a fully acknowledged member of their family. Rebecca Miller is married to another Daniel – Daniel Day-Lewis – and is a writer herself. They are private people and don't do many media interviews, but Rebecca has spoken a little about her love for Daniel and the things he has been able to learn and the advances he has made.

March 21 has been designated Down Syndrome Day, launched by the late Jerome Lejeune, who discovered Trisomy 21 – the chromosomal disorder which causes Down syndrome. This Frenchman unfailingly championed the humanity, and abilities, of people with Down syndrome. Older people will remember that there was a time when a child with Down syndrome was not only hidden from the world but also regarded as a person of no potential – simply a child who would never develop. I once interviewed Professor Lejeune – in the 1980s – and he was eager to emphasise back then that a child with Down syndrome was no cause for shame and that children with the syndrome often have much more ability and potential than is realised. He pioneered that view.

The story of Daniel Miller is an illumination of Professor Lejeune's insight that people with Down syndrome are an essential part of our human family.

Cultures Vary – Each Has Its Strengths

I was impressed by the bright, articulate young woman who was assigned to me in working on a book project. We did our professional work together and then, as women so often do – thankfully – we turned to discussing family, friends and our personal situations. She was Irish but had previously lived for more than a decade in Germany, an experience she much enjoyed. 'I didn't really emigrate for economic reasons,' she said. 'It was more that – well, I felt Ireland was a rather restrictive society in many ways.'

This would have been in the 1990s. She felt, especially, that Ireland was still too much of a closed society when it came to sex and sexuality. 'What I liked about Germany was that people were much more open about sex. More candid, more honest and less inhibited.' She liked that attitude and it was one of the liberating aspects, she found, of living in Germany.

And then her father grew ill and eventually died. She had always been close to her dad and his loss brought much grief. She returned to Ireland just as he was dying and she remained until after the funeral. And she found that when it came to death Irish culture was open, candid, comforting and graceful. Nobody felt inhibited about mentioning death, and the rituals of mourning were fully embraced. Goodbyes were said with an open coffin and, hard though that was, it was somehow cathartic – even liberating.

She went back to her job in Germany and found, among her circle of friends there, that death was a more difficult, even embarrassing, subject: people found it awkward to express their condolences or to speak openly and candidly about her bereavement. She got the impression that they just preferred to consign it to some private area of experience, ignore it and move on. She felt she couldn't talk to her German friends about the loss of her father and the way he had died.

After that she stopped disparaging her native Ireland for its attitudes to sex. There were compensations.

Cultures are different. It would be a poor world if we were all the same. We all criticise our native societies, but then events sometimes reveal to us that they also have their strengths.

Mother's Day

26 March

Several days around the globe are allocated for Mother's Day – it can be March, it can be May, as in America (and France). It is a nice idea to show respect to mothers, and which mother would turn down a special tribute? How lovely it is to receive a card or a greeting from a loving offspring on this day.

But on these mothers' days, perhaps we should sometimes think of the women throughout the ages for whom mothering was a penalty, and often an offence, punished by social ostracisation. The late Brian Sewell, art critic and sometimes acid, but always entertaining, commentator, wrote in a striking autobiography about the experience of being born out of wedlock in London in the 1930s and the price that was paid by both mother and child: 'It must be difficult now, well into the next century, for anyone to understand how sullying was the stigma of illegitimacy to both mother and child in 1931, the year of my birth,' he recalled.

'The blood relationships of the child were far less important than his legitimacy, and if this was not established by marriage, preferably before the event, then the child might well be taken from his mother's arms and despatched to those of adoptive parents or to the anonymity of the orphanage. The unmarried mother was without status; she dropped to the bottom of society's heap and her child might, for ever, be similarly marked for life with a birth certificate that betrayed him, denied him education, profession and, certainly, inheritance.'

His grandmother, a socialite and a friend of the aesthete Lord Clark (whose series *Civilisation* was a broadcasting epic in its time), would never have wanted any of her friends and peers to know that she had an 'illegitimate grandchild' and Brian Sewell was often shunned because of the status of his birth. When he was three, his maternal grandmother and his aunt Jessica both died: his mother was not even informed of these deaths by her unreconciled father. 'There remained no hope of support, emotional, familial or financial other than the tiny monthly stipend from my father's mother, whom we never saw or communicated with again.' He and his mother lived 'in ill-furnished rooms in basements and attics, a few weeks here, a few more there, some of which we left in the middle of the night, whisper quiet, tip-toe treading, wearing as much of our clothing as we could, not bundled against the cold, but for easier carrying, the rent unpaid …'

Thus it was for a mother in times gone by, who bore her child with remarkable courage – she was offered money to have the pregnancy aborted, but refused, in the face of public stigma.

Motherhood hasn't always been a bed of roses.

Duty Calls

It's a dreary Bank Holiday Monday, and I know what I ought to do. I ought to go and visit a friend who is confined to a care home because of a stroke. I don't really want to do this: it seems like a bit of a painful duty, and he's not really a close friend, and I'm not sure I have anything much to say to him. But two things nag at my conscience: one is that I was instructed, in my youth, to perform 'the corporal works of mercy'. Christians were enjoined to visit the sick (and those in prison), and I believe there was an indulgence attached to such an action – that is, you might be let off some stretch of time in Purgatory by accomplishing such merciful deeds. I take this, perhaps, to be in the manner of an incentive to what was also known as 'Christian charity'.

But, hey, there's a good movie on locally, and I'd rather take myself off to see that. Then I recall the Sunday rule of my growing years. The children in our neighbourhood used to have a Sunday afternoon matinée at the local cinema; it was always a treat, and something to look forward too. But if you announced in the morning that you didn't feel well enough to go to church, then you would be told you were not well enough to go to the pictures. First duty, then treats.

The second nagging feeling I have is that I have seen what it is like for people who are alone in care homes and may be unvisited, and I know from experience how much a visit can be appreciated.

Much as I feel reluctant to bestir myself to get out of the house, get into the car and drive to the location, I know I'll feel a sense of guilt and self-reproach if I don't do so. I'll feel disappointed in myself that I haven't done something that I should do.

Was that French cynic La Rochefoucauld right when he claimed that even in our most meritorious deeds there is an element of self-interest? That we do everything essentially for ourselves, rather than others? Perhaps.

I go, all the same. He appreciates the visit. I'm glad I made the effort.

Sex ...

One of the advantages of old age is that people can lose interest in sex. Not all individuals do. As an advice dispenser to *The Oldie* magazine, I know that there are plenty of folk in their sixties, seventies, eighties and even beyond still keen on 'dating' and finding a companion who is also a lover. Men who lose their wives often write about the need for a companion in bed, and not just for companionship.

But for others – and I include myself in this – the Greek philosopher who said 'To lose sexual desire is like being unchained from a maniac' got it about right. To paraphrase Oscar Wilde's witticism about the problem of socialism, sexual desire takes up far too much of one's evenings. Falling in love can be a kind of madness – you take leave of your senses, in order, perhaps, to gratify your senses. You make a complete fool of yourself, frequently with the wrong people. Recklessness, lack of judgement, demented attacks of jealousy can all go into the mix. How liberating it is to be free of such headstrong and irrational urges and to be able to focus on calmer pastimes that emerge as much more rewarding.

I've heard some of my contemporaries – passionate and ardent people in their youth – now, in old age, express a kind of disgust for the sexual functions of the flesh. 'Yuck! The very thought of all that horrible squishy flesh rubbing!' That's nature protecting us from the fires of desire, or perhaps the perils of looking vulnerable or pathetic in decrepitude. The danger, for the elderly asexual, is to grow moralistic or finger-wagging about explicit sexuality. It is not our place to disapprove of the young and fiery who are living through their passionate and ardent years. It is our place to reserve our judgement and to see the whole picture in perspective: sexuality also brings pleasure, love, unity – and, above all, perhaps, the joy of procreation and new life.

Old people often don't much like the amount of explicit sexuality which is apparently obligatory nowadays in movies and TV dramas. Watching actors pretending to engage in sexual intercourse only recalls Lord Chesterfield's axiom: 'The pleasure is momentary and the position ridiculous,' and historical dramas have been spoiled for me by all the fake grunting and gasping.

Isn't it strange? We who once called for sexual liberation now often find other diversions far more interesting!

... And Money

Sex was approached with decorum in polite society until, perhaps, the 1960s. Parts of the body were not given frank anatomical descriptions: a book was banned in Ireland in the 1940s because it contained the word 'breast'. And I was quite taken aback when I heard an American scriptwriter use the word 'penis' in public, circa 1966. Others must have been too, as there was a ripple of nervous giggling.

Any soap opera or movie set before 1960 which mentions the word 'pregnant' has not done its lexical research. It was not a word in regular circulation, and it usually related to the farmyard.

Funnily, another area of respectable decorum was money. Only vulgar people spoke about the price of things. A woman in our neighbourhood was regarded as 'common' because she bragged about the cost of every item in her new home.

'So nouveau riche,' was one judgement.

'No class,' went another.

Yeats captured perfectly the mentality of the Irish refined classes when he scorned 'Biddy's pence and Paudeen's ha'pence' and the distasteful reality of the 'greasy till'.

Yet people weren't unaware of money. Entire dynasties were constructed on the principle of the dowry. The most respectable of women kept hidden savings accounts. When my Connemara grandmother died in the 1940s, she was found to have six secret post-office accounts with small deposits in each.

A married woman couldn't have a bank account without the menfolk in her family knowing – a man had to countersign bank documents. But she could have a post-office account, which she might maintain in utter discretion. It was always nice to know that there was a small nest-egg maturing somewhere in case of a pressing need.

The lore of the grandmothers was passed down through the ages, and one motto from this matriarchal vein was: 'Never tell your husband everything. Especially about money.' As many men did not divulge their incomes to their wives, this seemed fair.

Another piece of women's wisdom transmitted by Irishwomen down the generations was the proper attitude of a bride to her husband's assets. My aunty Dorothy believed that a woman's attitude to her husband's revenue should be: 'What's thine is mine; but what's mine is my own.'

As with sex, the fact that it wasn't considered quite proper to speak about money didn't mean that people didn't think about it. Sometimes they thought about nothing else, which you could infer from hints and allusions in adult conversation.

And as with sex, money might be clothed in euphemisms: wealth was referred to as 'means'. Despite the lack of open discussion, it was evident that money was important, just as it was obvious that sex was exciting. But still, to give the price of anything was vulgar. And to be mean with money was the lowest of the low. Better a man who squandered the family income on every kind of carousing than one considered 'tight-fisted'.

My sister dumped a boyfriend who seemed to have a promising bank career because, when a restaurant bill was presented, he studied it, checked the arithmetic and even queried an item. Meanie!

In our world today everyone talks, non-stop, about money. The economy is everything. The only nostalgia I have for pre-modern financial values was that the currency itself seemed so solid. An old penny was something of substance: a half-a-crown was a fabulous piece of silver you held in your hand. We weren't educated about money, but we could feel something of its power in the very coins in our pockets.

Change is Good

I've very often been asked the question – so often that it bores me rigid to hear it repeated – 'Why did you change from being a wild child and a bad girl in the 1960s and 1970s into a right-wing Catholic subsequently?' I'm tempted to put 'right-wing Catholic' in quotes because that's somebody else's definition of me and not my own definition of myself, and one of the prevailing rules of self-worth is that you should never allow yourself to be defined by someone else.

But change isn't complicated. Times change. You change. You grow up; you grow old. You acquire property, children, responsibilities; you begin to reflect on some of the consequences of your more rash decisions and to consider that those who do not learn from their mistakes go on repeating them. Not that everything I did in my youth was a mistake – all of life is a mixture of good and bad – but there were some wild times which were indeed *folies de la jeunesse*.

All lives have to be seen within the context of their time. I became a teenager in the 1950s, which was, by anyone's measure, and for most societies, an almost intolerably stuffy age. It was more rigid in Ireland than elsewhere because the Republic of Ireland had been neutral in the Second World War and had been sealed off from the social changes that occurred in other societies because of that momentous event. So in Ireland the 1950s were really more like a direct continuation of the 1930s. In some ways we hadn't got out of the Victorian era. Why wouldn't our generation want to rebel and cut loose? It would have been remarkably dopey not to.

But the world went from remarkable – sometimes great – literature being banned to full-frontal everything on the Internet; it went from punishing unmarried mothers to the jovial suggestion that abortion should be celebrated as a sacrament; it went from regarding cigarettes as calming for the nerves to shrieking abuse at anyone who so much as vaped. Values changed. And why would those of us who have lived through such changes not have altered and developed and revised our lifestyles also? Saul Bellow went from Trotskyist to neo-conservative; Wordsworth went from republican revolutionary to nature-conserving monarchist. Those of us who change can feel we're in good company.

A Manner of Speaking

Paraprosdokians are figures of speech in which the latter part of a sentence or phrase is surprising or unexpected and is frequently humorous. (Winston Churchill loved them.)

1. Where there's a will, I want to be in it.
2. The last thing I want to do is hurt you ... but it's still on my list.
3. Since light travels faster than sound, some people appear bright until you hear them speak.
4. If I agreed with you, we'd both be wrong.
5. We never really grow up – we only learn how to act in public.
6. War does not determine who is right, only who is left.
7. Knowledge is knowing a tomato is a fruit. Wisdom is not putting it in a fruit salad.
8. To steal ideas from one person is plagiarism. To steal from many is research.
9. I didn't say it was your fault, I said I was blaming you.
10. In filling out an application, where it says, 'In case of emergency, notify ...' I answered 'a doctor'.
11. Women will never be equal to men until they can walk down the street with a bald head and a beer gut and still think they are sexy.
12. You do not need a parachute to skydive. You only need a parachute to skydive twice.

13. I used to be indecisive, but now I'm not so sure.
14. To be sure of hitting the target, shoot first and call whatever you hit the target.
15. Going to church doesn't make you a Christian, any more than standing in a garage makes you a car.
16. You're never too old to learn something stupid.
17. I'm supposed to respect my elders, but it's getting harder and harder for me to find one now.

The person who sent me this message on Facebook added: 'Spread the laughter, share the cheer, let's be happy while we're here.'

Quite so!

A Chinese Superstition

4 April

There was a time when a lady might conceal her age: when we asked our elders what age they were, they would reply, gnomically, 'As old as my tongue and older than my teeth.' Today, we are all a lot more open about our date of birth – because we have to be. It is part of our identity, registered every time we fill in a form, and easily checked out on the Internet. I'm utterly accustomed to giving my date of birth, which is 4/4/44, and equally accustomed to people responding by saying, 'Oh! All the fours!' Yes, all the fours, which, as it turns out, is a very bad omen in China, since four is their unlucky number – the equivalent of our thirteen, only probably more significant, since Chinese culture has many superstitions about signs and numbers.

So you can imagine I didn't get a very warm welcome when I visited China: eyes opened wide as my passport was examined – 4/4/44! Not just one four, but four fours – how unlucky can that be? I was virtually shunned. I had been booked into a hotel in Beijing by the newspaper that sent me there, but there was some reluctance to accommodate me, and I had to make a fuss, which was also considered unseemly, as the Chinese, understandably, dislike it when Westerners – who probably seem to them lumpy, with huge noses and a habit of immodesty – start shouting at them. But even the bearer of the unlucky four has to sleep for the night, and eventually a bed was provided.

Other people's superstitions seem, at best, quaint and, at worst, malign and backward, and the curse of four meant nothing to me. As I prepared to depart from Beijing airport, I was escorted towards the aircraft by several officials – I was late checking in and everyone seemed to be anxious to get me on that flight. And in the end, I was relieved to depart too. No one likes being seen as an unlucky person; although, all things considered, I have not been particularly unlucky in my lifetime.

But turn any stigma around, say I: if others think it's unlucky to bear the 4/4/44, then do the opposite and bear it with pride!

People-Pleasing

'People-pleasing' is warned against in every kind of therapy. It's seen as a kind of weakness of character that leads us to do things for the sake of others, rather than by our own choice. And this means we are, effectively, leading our lives on others' terms, rather than on our own.

Despite being quite a headstrong and egotistical sort of person, I find I do quite a lot of people-pleasing, when I examine my record. To take a trivial example, I don't really like crowded parties – chit-chat with strangers (whom I can barely hear because of the decibel level) bores me. And as I don't drink alcohol, I grow even more bored by consuming endless glasses of water, since few hosts or hostesses provide anything very imaginative for non-drinkers. (Coca-Cola, cold and lemoned, would be a start, and this is not a product placement but a sincere recommendation.) Yet I weakly agree to attend such soirées because of my urge towards people-pleasing. I feel I shouldn't be disobliging. It might be rude. And then people might think I'm horrid.

This is, obviously, a form of vanity and popularity-seeking. We don't want to be disliked. We don't want to offend. We don't want to be described as a crabby old witch who is notoriously difficult to please and anti-social. We crave approval.

The therapists are surely right when they say that we should be more self-affirming about our own social choices: we should do those things that we choose to do and have the self-confidence to turn down those things that we really do not want to do. But they're only right in moderation. Human beings are social animals. Few individuals are born to be recluses. Social intercourse requires a certain level of reciprocity, and that means that sometimes you do, quite naturally, feel obliged to engage in a social event just to please the folks who asked you. Anyway, you can always be surprised. You can dread having to turn up at some gig and end up having a very interesting time.

It's when people-pleasing affects the major decisions of life that it may be regarded as dysfunctional: marrying to please one's family, changing jobs to please, or appease, a spouse, moving countries to please the boss. When the motive is to please others in big decisions, it may well impair or undermine one's own self-worth. Sometimes we should indeed just please ourselves.

Mother Earth Day

22 April

I love the idea that our planet Earth is a perfect environment because it is in 'the Goldilocks zone'. We remember the story of Goldilocks and the Three Bears: when the said little girl with golden hair entered the cottage of the three bears, she tested out their chairs, their porridge and their beds. Her judgement on these items usually emerged that one was too big and one was too small, but one was just right; one was too hot and one was too cold, but one was just right; one was too hard and one was too soft, but the middle one was just right. And thus did Goldilocks boldly make herself at home when she found conditions that were just right.

And so with planet Earth. It's not too hot, like Venus, and it's not too cold, like Neptune: it's just right. It's not too big, like Jupiter, and it's not too small, like Pluto, it's just right. It's not too near to the sun, nor too far from the sun: its orbit of twenty-four hours is just perfect for human habitation, as is almost every other aspect of its composition. Earth is altogether a perfect Goldilocks zone, where everything is just right. Aren't we lucky?

Those responsive to the environment have always appreciated the beauty and order of the natural world produced by this Earth of ours, but perhaps it was the first clear pictures of planet Earth taken from space – in 1968 and then in 1972 – from the Apollo space crafts that brought home to us just what a dear little place this Earth is. Sir Fred Hoyle, the astronomer, predicted right back in the 1940s that pictures of Earth from space would change our relationship with the planet, and so it has proved. As the pictures became universal, so a concern for Earth's environment grew, and the ecology movement became as important as – or perhaps more important than – the space programme.

Those who love to learn about space often suggest that there must be other planets similar to Earth out there in the infinity of galaxies. Perhaps. But so far, Earth is the only Goldilocks zone we have, and its unending wonders and beauty should daily inspire our awe.

The Truth in Fable

I love fables and following are two of my favourites.

The first is a Yiddish fable about a man who is told in a dream to search for a precious stone which is rightfully his. He lives in a village in western Ukraine and duly sets off to find the gem in question. He travels to Poland, through the forests of Germany, to Italy and throughout the Balkans, but can never find the stone that has been promised to him. He treks through Bulgaria and Romania and throughout central Europe until he eventually arrives back in his home village.

Disappointed at the fruitlessness of his long search, he sits down by his fireside and lights a pipe. Gazing into the hearth, he sees something glittering in the recess of the chimney. He begins to poke around and uncovers a small fireproof box. He takes it out and opens it – and there lies the precious emerald stone that he learned about in a dream.

The moral of the fable is that sometimes we go all around the world in search of something, and it is not until we have been through all our travails that we see it is right there close to home, before our very eyes.

The second fable is one told by the economic commentator Martin Wolf in the *Financial Times*.

A man who is condemned to death beseeches the king for a pardon – offering to teach the royal horse to sing. The king is sceptical but agrees to allow the condemned man a stay of execution for a year – but by the end of the year, the horse must be able to sing.

The offender's cellmate scoffs, saying, 'You know you can never teach that horse to sing!' But the man replies, 'I now have a year I didn't have previously and no one can predict what may happen in a year. The king might die; the horse might die; I might die. And the horse might sing!'

Who knows what the future may bring: and time may bring a solution to your greatest headache.

Priority, Please!

Youth is surely a formative time, and the things that happen to you in youth stay with you – and return to you later, too, sometimes with a revised understanding.

When I was an eighteen-year-old au pair in Paris, I was travelling one day on an underground Metro train in which all the seats were taken. A woman of about thirty got on, hand-in-hand with quite a young child. She immediately took out an identifying document of some kind in a plastic holder and showed it to a seated young man. '*Priorité, s'il vous plait,*' she said to him quite firmly. He duly stood up and ceded her his seat.

Fresh from Ireland, I was astonished, and even embarrassed, by this scene. Imagine having the nerve to ask for a seat on a train! Imagine whipping out your papers, as bold as brass, and proving you have 'priority'! In Ireland, you'd rather die on your feet than ask someone for their seat; as for proving that you were entitled to it – gosh, it's so forward!

Shouldn't you wait to be offered such privileges?

All these years later, however, I think the woman's attitude was absolutely right and showed due confidence about her entitlements. If she was the mother of a young child (she might even have been pregnant as well), why shouldn't she expect that some healthy-looking young fellow give her a seat? And why shouldn't she demand, as of right, a 'priority'? Good for her!

I notice, now, that some trains in Kent are introducing a card whereby a traveller may indeed demand to be allowed to sit on one of the priority seats set aside for older people, people with special needs or people with a disability. For reasons of various broken-down parts of my anatomy, as well as age (Seán Mac Réamoinn compared himself in old age to an Irish census form: 'broken down by age, sex and religion'), I think I shall acquire one. But will I have the nerve to whip it out – with a flourish, if I recall correctly – calling out 'Priority, please!' as that Frenchwoman did all those years ago? Maybe not. I'll probably sidle up to the seat occupier and very apologetically begin, 'Look, I'm terribly sorry to disturb you, but ...' Influences are important, but how much can you really change your basic character?

Counting Your Blessings – It's Complicated!

We are told – wisely – that we should count our blessings, make a list of the things we should be thankful for, develop 'an attitude of gratitude'. I try to bear this in mind, but it does go against human nature sometimes.

Once we are in possession of something, we take it for granted. Once we get what we want, we seldom cast our minds back to the time when we didn't have it, because we now want something else. Am I grateful for the food that is on my table, for the shelter over my head, for the family connections that I benefit from, for the car at my door which can take me anywhere (and the wherewithal to fill it with petrol), for the fact that I am still alive when others, more deserving than I – others who didn't smoke, drink or carouse away a mis-spent youth – have not survived into old age?

For the most part, I am not. I am far more likely to grumble and complain about what I don't have. I have food on the table but, drat it, there's the bore of shopping for it and cooking it. I have a roof over my head, but a house, I reflect, is a little like a demanding and peevish mistress – always needing attention, maintenance and restoration. The family? Worry, worry, worry. Alive, yes, but shall I count the aches and pains, the minor disabilities from eye trouble to shortness of breath?

It's only when something happens that gratitude is triggered. The National Health Service carries out a biannual test for bowel cancer and, having carried out such a test on me, informs me that the test is satisfactory: I do not have bowel cancer (though it could show up the next time). Neither, for the moment, do I have lung cancer, according to a chest X-ray. So be grateful, I tell myself.

Reverting to the household, we had trouble recently with the radiators and the hot water because of problems with the cylinder and the tank. It would cost a lot to repair and I had to budget carefully to find the cash (and find the plumber too). For two months in a cold spring, we had no hot running water, as in days of old. Finally, the funds were found, the plumber was appointed and a new cylinder was put in place and we had the joy of hot running water once again. Oh, joy! Truly 'you do not miss the water until the well runs dry'. And within a few weeks, I never gave it another thought.

The Easter Rising

24 April

Modern nations – even ancient nations – often need a 'founding myth', and for the Republic of Ireland, the events of 1916 fulfil that with poetic exactitude. Here was a rising led by a dissonant group of poets, dreamers, visionaries, hardened old Fenians, driven Communists and patriotic rebels who had little chance against the might of the British Empire: and thereby, they duly met their deaths by execution.

In the midst of the mass slaughter occurring on the Western Front, the execution of fifteen (subsequently sixteen, when Roger Casement was hanged for treason) men was not numerically significant. But symbols – and founding myths – aren't about numbers: they are about stories that we tell ourselves over and over again so that they become interwoven into a collective identity.

The executions of the Easter Rising rebels ensured that the myth became embedded: the images of James Connolly, too wounded to stand, facing a firing squad strapped to a chair; Joseph Plunkett, the consumptive poet with a face like St Francis; and Seán Mac Diarmada, the polio-stricken tram worker, sharing his last Woodbine cigarette while saying the Rosary in his condemned cell, seem too beautifully romantic not to become legends.

Who could die better than Connolly, the old Marxist, taking Holy Communion and telling his wife: 'Wasn't it a full life, Lillie, and isn't this a good end?' The English soldiers accompanying these men to their deaths were themselves often moved to honour and respect for them. As Ruth Dudley Edwards shows in her wonderful book about the signatories of the Easter Rising, *The Seven*, these men were not really a band of conspirators: they were individuals who moved in similar circles in the heady era of the Celtic Renaissance – the early 1900s – and, then, it seemed, inexorably, towards one another. But they were very different characters.

Patrick Pearse was a perceptive schoolmaster (and would have made a brilliant journalist: the Proclamation is a great piece of rhetorical writing), ultra-Catholic visionary and, in Ruth's analysis, a tormented and repressed paedophile who wrote poetry to the beauty of young boys. Tom Clarke was a veteran Fenian, an old dynamiter who had served long, hard years in English prisons and been well toughened by the experience. Connolly was a Communist and trade union activist from the Edinburgh slums. Thomas MacDonagh came from a cultivated family of schoolteachers: he was a star pupil, a nature lover, an accomplished musician and a poet with a special admiration for Jane Austen. Joseph Plunkett's father was a papal count and his mother a mad eccentric who neglected her children but gave to philanthropic causes. Mac Diarmada came from a modest background in Co. Leitrim and had been fired as a tram conductor for smoking a cigarette during a break – very contemporary, indeed. Eamonn Ceannt (*né* Kent) was a shy but fanatical Irish-language enthusiast with a spotless domestic life.

What they came to share in common – with the exception of Tom Clarke, the old Fenian who never healed his quarrel with the

Church – was a sense of Catholic self-sacrifice. Another shared value was their strong commitment to the teetotal movement. These Irishmen abhorred alcohol!

Their idealism was inspiring. Pearse remains a fascinating character study – a man of essential kindness and gentleness. He certainly became infected by 'war fever' by 1914, but didn't everyone? Connolly's initial objectives were thoroughly decent – why shouldn't working people have fair pay, state pensions, a minimum wage, children's allowance, free education and a forty-eight-hour working week? He and Lillie kept having children they couldn't really afford, but they loved them all and struggled to support them.

The peripheral figure of Yeats hovers around the scenario – always picking up the zeitgeist but always helpful to those poets, such as MacDonagh, who were lesser talents than he.

Theirs was surely an honourable legacy, and the Proclamation of the Irish Republic was remarkably progressive and inclusive, for its time: it stood as a basis for the Irish Constitution, which is a magnificent document of human rights, citizens' duties and sensitivity to the culture of which it is the heir and the guardian.

Four Ducks on a Pond

William Allingham (1824–1889)

Four ducks on a pond,
A grass-bank beyond,
A blue sky of spring,
White clouds on the wing;
What a little thing
To remember for years –
To remember with tears.

In my childhood, we would often recite the Donegal poet William Allingham's enchanting verse 'The Faeries', which went 'Up the airy mountain / Down the rushy glen / We daren't go a-hunting / For fear of little men'. It draws on Irish country lore about 'the little people' (leprechauns and the like, who were traditionally rather evil spirits, not the cuddly creatures as represented in gift-shops these days). Allingham, born in Ballyshannon, Co. Donegal, worked as a customs officer in Belfast, the Isle of Man and New Ross, Co. Wexford, but was encouraged in his early writings by Leigh Hunt. He came to know many renowned London literary personalities, including Tennyson, Carlyle and the pre-Raphaelite circle (Burne-Jones, Millais and Rossetti), and eventually settled in London. At the age of fifty he married and his wife, Helen Allingham, was a noted watercolour painter (who herself enjoyed a revival in the 1980s, having earlier been dismissed as producing works that were 'too pretty') and a faithful keeper of his legacy after he died in Hampstead in 1889. 'Four Ducks on a Pond' is only twenty-one words long, but it evokes such a strong picture glimpsed in childhood, remaining in the inner eye for the rest of the poet's life. Born into the Church of Ireland, Allingham had a deep interest in Gaelic and Catholic traditions, even once visiting Lough Derg as a place of pilgrimage, and W. B. Yeats was influenced by his subjects and imagery.

Summer

Wild Nights

Emily Dickinson (1830–1866)

Wild nights! Wild nights!
Were I with thee,
Wild nights should be
Our luxury.

Futile the wins
To a heart in port –
Done with the compass,
Done with the chart.

Rowing in Eden!
Ah! The sea!
Might I but moor
Tonight in thee!

We know almost nothing about the source of this deeply felt poem, since Emily Dickinson's private life remains a mystery. She was the daughter of a US congressman from a patrician family in Massachusetts; her father was domineering and probably controlling, but he did encourage education for his two daughters as well as his son. Emily lived the life of a virtual recluse, and no one knows who inspired the yearning that 'Wild Nights' expresses. She wrote about seventeen hundred poems, and they would never be known to posterity if her sister Lavinia hadn't conserved, collected and had them published. She received little encouragement from an editor to whom she sent them. Miss Dickinson, who nearly always wore white, felt much haunted by death – Victorians were well acquainted with loss – and died at fifty-six of Bright's disease. Her poem on the theme of death, 'Because I Could Not Stop for Death', is a great classic. She is now regarded as a feminist icon and a poet of unusual originality. But if it hadn't been for her sister's devotion, we might never have heard of her at all.

Buddha Day

21 May

The philosopher Arthur Schopenhauer believed that instead of men addressing one another as Monsieur, Sir or Mein Herr, they should hail each other as 'My fellow-sufferer' or '*compagnon de misères*'. It would help us to remind one another that the whole of life is 'a disappointment … a cheat'. Work, worry, labour and trouble 'form the lot of almost all men their whole life long'. Misfortune in general is the rule of the species, he believed.

Suffering is 'the direction and object of life' for Schopenhauer. 'If children were brought into the world by an act of pure reason alone, would the human race continue to exist?' he asks. (He was a single man – grumpy old bachelor would not be inaccurate – childless and more or less without any surviving family connections.) His general outlook, I think it's fair to say, was, as he admits, 'comfortless', even misanthropic.

It's a surprise to learn, then, that the same Schopenhauer was inclined towards Buddhism – especially surprising to those of us who think of Buddhism as a nice Hollywood-lite kind of religion, strong on environmentalism and lacking in the sense of sin (and guilt) of Judeo-Christianity. Yet true Buddhism, though it emphasises the wholeness of all creation, does not flinch from the dark side, for the Buddha's first dictum is that 'Life is suffering'. Buddhist teaching also emphasises that the origin of suffering is a craving for sensuality, the acquisition of identity or the fear of annihilation, which I take to be too much ego and possibly too much appetite for sex. Schopenhauer believed the Brahma text which explained that the world originated in a 'kind of fall', which is not too far from Genesis.

By the way, the gloomy Schopenhauer was very fond of animals, which is surely an engaging aspect of his character.

Buddhism is a very old form of faith, originating with the Gautama Buddha, more than four centuries before Christ. Many sages and wise people through the centuries have studied and followed the Buddha and become Buddhist monks and nuns. (Pleasingly, you can also become a Buddhist monk on a temporary basis – say, take it on for a couple of years and then return to civil life.)

And despite the emphasis on suffering, there is also a belief that we must seek the middle way between extreme asceticism and self-indulgent hedonism – that 'golden mean' found in Greek (and inherited by Judeo-Christian) philosophy.

Africa Day

25 May

It's a grand idea to hold an international Africa Day to celebrate the positive things about the African continent. It is too often associated with catastrophes and disasters; and, indeed, Africa has been unlucky, if you like, in some of the elements associated with its climate. Tropical diseases are a curse and the tsetse fly is responsible for many afflictions all over that continent.

But there are many other sides to African life. When I visited Africa, I noticed that African babies seldom cried, unless they were sick. I also observed how Africans love style and fashion – at a UN world conference for women, the African women were by far the most stunning to look at.

I caught a glimpse of the opening of parliament ceremonial in, I think, Rwanda, as transmitted by a French television crew, and it looked absolutely fabulous. What elegance and *joie de vivre* in a nation which has experienced such suffering.

I remember attending a Catholic Mass in Beijing during that UN conference. The Chinese authorities allowed it, but it had to be held in the discreet backroom of a rather anonymous building. It proceeded with some reverence, and then, suddenly, the African women began to sing. It was as if birds of paradise had formed a chorus, and they brought to the service a most beautiful sense of musical spirituality: they lifted it to something soaring with natural harmony. This wasn't planned; it just happened spontaneously and it was truly memorable.

Afterwards, there were refreshments – mostly tea – and many of the women present spoke of having been taught by an Irish nun, priest or brother. This could be applied universally – Irish missions were once called Ireland's spiritual empire (with some pride) – but it was especially applicable to Africa.

There are deposits of Irish cultural investment from the past all over Africa. The Medical Missionaries of Mary, founded in Drogheda in 1936 by Mother Mary Martin, virtually pioneered mother-and-child care in the African bush. The MMMs were, at the start, nun–doctors, who, by the 1940s were also taking flying lessons. In Sierra Leone, the Irish Holy Ghost Fathers set up a fine education system and left it in mint condition at the point of decolonisation. Edel Quinn, the Irish mystic, travelled through Africa, north to south, lodging at all times with Irish nuns, often Dominicans. The Dominican order in South Africa ran racially integrated schools even during the apartheid regime. Ireland, indeed, has many strong links with Africa.

Bag Lady

When Christine Lagarde, the boss of the International Monetary Fund, was pictured carrying an Hermès Kelly handbag (estimated to cost €7,000) while meeting Taoiseach Enda Kenny, social media was awash with objections to her accessory of choice.

It was angrily pointed out that €7,000 would go a long way in funding benefits for one of the many families in Ireland in dire financial straits. The conspicuous consumption of Marie Antoinette herself was quickly ascribed to Madame Lagarde.

Those of us who are handbag addicts – an incorrigible compulsion – couldn't but be drawn to the exquisite design and fabrication of the handbag. Didn't William Morris say that we should seek to own only that which is either beautiful or useful? A well-designed handbag is both beautiful and useful.

But wait! Is it tactful for the wealthy elite to flaunt their expensive possessions, especially when they have been in a position to recommend austerity?

Then again, by purchasing such a handbag, doesn't the lady give employment to leather workers, designers, retail assistants and those toiling in the fashion industry?

Indeed, a struggle of conscience.

Oh, handbag addictions. Those who are prey to it will know what I am talking about. I have to restrain myself from buying handbags: surely, I have enough? Yes, but never quite the ideal one! Life might be said to be the eternal search for the perfect handbag.

I'm sure this is a psychological problem, linked with fantasy. The addict always imagines that a new handbag will change everything. A perfect handbag will mean immaculate organisation and a magically organised mind.

And then handbags in recent years have blossomed enormously as a design item. The addict can hardly be blamed.

Because, like all typical addicts, she finds a reason to blame someone else – that's characteristic: it's always someone else's fault. It may indeed be the fault of human nature. Even in Communist China, the playwright Arthur Miller observed, the lure of the bazaar was never far from the human psyche – with all its transformative promises. If I were rewriting the Book of Genesis, I'd suggest that the serpent tempt Eve with a heavenly handbag.

The novelist Barbara Taylor Bradford confessed to being a handbag addict at the age of eighty-one, owning twenty-four Hermès bags, five Chanels and thirty designer evening bags, all of which she likes to describe in great detail. And though her Chanel bags cost about £1,975 each, she still also likes to find a 'bargain' bag.

We baggy addicts feel that if Christine Lagarde has found her perfect handbag, even with a price tag of €7,000, then it's surely a price worth paying.

No Smoking Day

11 March

The stigmatisation of smoking cigarettes is perhaps one of the most remarkable reversals of values in our time. I recently saw a young mother walking through the park, pushing a buggy with one hand and in the other holding the cigarette she was smoking. The thought suggested itself that it probably won't be long before such behaviour is actually illegal, and any such young woman will be tapped on the shoulder by a member of the constabulary.

Yet, but a short time ago, almost everyone seemed to smoke: there was smoking on buses, on trains, on airplanes and in the cinema. Lighting up a fag was a friendly kind of thing to do, and a way of sharing collegiality and comradeship. When Opus Dei first started in Spain in 1936, a priest had to be selected to embark on the habit of smoking, since it was calculated that no man could ever identify with the working class unless he smoked like working men. After the Second World War, in the ruins of the German Reich, cigarettes became the only reliable currency for a time, and reports suggest that everyone was desperate for a gasper.

The fag was an accessory in many a twentieth-century movie, and the most arresting aspect of *Casablanca* – my favourite film of all time – is just how much Humphrey Bogart smoked; and I can't overlook the fact that the habit killed him. King George VI told the Irish envoy John Dulanty that he dreaded getting through his coronation service without a ciggie – and the ciggies killed him too.

Eventually, the generation that smoked was nagged, nudged or propelled into quitting (or else they died off, sometimes from smoking), and it was forbidden to think of smoking as glamorous (as it was when Marlene Dietrich was filmed through a haze of smoke), friendly or a sign of progress and maturity. Neither was it feminist, although 'the right to smoke' was an issue for women in the 1920s, and in the 1970s a brand of cigarettes was specifically aimed at women, telling them 'You've come a long way, baby'. For the sake of our health and the health of children, no doubt it is better that the cigarette has gone the way of the spittoon and the casual dose of laudanum. Cigarettes have even been airbrushed from the mouths of men who smoked like chimneys, like Albert Camus on French stamps.

And yet, when all is said and done, it was a pleasure. An unhealthy pleasure for which a high price was paid. But a pleasure just the same: that first drag of a Gitane sent a direct, exquisite hit to that endomorphin spot of the brain. 'Take what you like,' says God, in a Spanish proverb. 'And pay for it.' Oh yes!

May-Time Beauty

I was driving through a stretch of countryside in the last week of May and, passing by fields where the grass was being mown, I had the urge to halt the car, get out and just lie in the grass, smelling the freshness of the air, hearing the birds, gazing on the trees, being in touch with nature. Such beautiful lilac and wisteria lining the country roads, as well as horse chestnuts, hawthorn (known as the May bush) and elderflower. The gorse was bright on the hills, and in the fields were buttercups, daisies and wild bluebells. Everything suddenly seemed so freshly flowering and abundant.

But I didn't halt the car and alight. I hurried on, mindful of some footling household chores I had to attend to: get to the supermarket, buy petrol, send my emails. Later, those thoughtful lines by the Welsh poet William Henry Davies came back to me:

What is this life, if full of care,
We have no time to stop and stare.
No time to stand beneath the boughs
And stare as long as sheep or cows.
No time to see, when woods we pass,
Where squirrels hide their nuts in grass.
No time to see, in broad daylight,
Streams full of stars, like skies at night ...

A poor life this if, full of care,
We have no time to stand and stare.

W. H. Davies had much time to stand and stare. Raised by his grandparents in Monmouthshire, he bought himself a cheap passage to the United States in the 1890s and lived as a tramp, sometimes riding the railroads. He said his education was picking up knowledge 'among tramps … on cattle boats and in common lodging houses'. Later he would try panning for gold in the Klondike and had to have his leg amputated below the knee after jumping from a train. In England he lived as a pedlar and street preacher, but he always wrote poetry (novels and memoir too), and would perhaps never have been known but for the support of George Bernard Shaw and Shaw's wife, Charlotte. He found love and marriage at the age of fifty-two.

Thank you, W. H. Davies, for your wise words. I must, must find more time to stand and stare, especially in the beauty of the May-time countryside.

Joan of Arc – All Things to the French

30 May

More movies have probably been made about Joan of Arc than any other Frenchwoman from history. She's an amazing character and has retained an iconic position in French culture at every point in the political system: heroine to the wartime Resistance, avatar to the right-wing National Front. Whether or not you are a Christian believer – and George Bernard Shaw, who wrote the terrific play *St Joan*, was not – what she achieved was impressive. She was one of my girlhood heroines, and she should still be upheld as a role model for young women, for her courage, her self-belief, her purposefulness and her command of authority.

Perhaps she could be a role model for people who have not had the opportunity of an education but affirm their goals anyway. Joan was born in 1412 to pious but unlettered peasant parents in the village of Domrémy in Lorraine. When she was seventeen years old, she heard what she described as supernatural voices telling her to take up arms and lead the French army against the English, who occupied France at the time. How did this young girl persuade the King of France, Charles VII, to allow her to lead an army into battle – and to win those battles so successfully? Joan felt that God was guiding her, and in this she transmitted a sense of will and purpose to the king.

As we know, Joan was captured (by her fellow-French Burgundians), handed over to the English and tried by an ecclesiastical court. Again, although uneducated, she astonished the court with her fluency and her ability to answer articulately and evade the legalistic traps laid for her. (The evidence of her trial is still available.) Nonetheless, she was condemned to death, and tied to a pillar at the Vieux-Marché in Rouen and burned alive. Two priests held a crucifix before her eyes as she faced the flames.

Some modern interpretations of Joan's life might suggest that she had schizophrenia – hearing voices is a known symptom. But the historic record shows that Joan remained sane in her reasoning, rational in argument and mature in her judgements. She proved her mettle in every degree, and throughout the centuries since her martyrdom, on 30 May 1431, she has been an inspiration to French identity.

Deaf Sentence

In the years before she died, the singer Cilla Black had lamented that she was going deaf, and this was a great affliction. Perhaps she found it tormenting because she was a singer and she was particularly sensitive to sound. I am going deaf myself, so I can quite see that it is a vexation; but that's how I regard my increasing deafness – annoying, but not tragic.

Being hard of hearing is often more irritating to other people – repeating questions that someone doesn't hear the first time is maddening.

Yet there is something called 'selective hearing', because we don't just hear with our ears. We also hear with a process inside our brains. Strangely, too, those who are hard of hearing can sometimes pick up on something that interests them or that they weren't supposed to hear. 'My God, you're not saying she's pregnant, are you?' being a sudden response to an overheard conversation. 'How much did you say he left in that will?' they'd say, after you came off the telephone.

It's been well-observed that, on stage, hearing difficulties have often been treated as something funny; but blindness has never been thought of as comical.

The comedy element lies in the capacity for mishearing and droll misunderstandings. The novelist David Lodge, when going deaf himself, wrote a hilarious novel about a middle-aged man becoming deaf while his father moves towards death: it is adroitly named *Deaf Sentence* – the play on words encapsulating the mis-hearings. You wouldn't think that such a theme could be funny, but in Lodge's masterly hands, it really is.

I wouldn't want to make light of being deaf, and certainly profound deafness must be a trial. I can see that deafness could begin to lock you into a silent world, more cut off from the rest of society. Increasing deafness also makes you tetchy about modern diction. Why must they *mumble* so much? Why must they *elide their words* – running them all together confusingly? And some people – even some radio professionals – *drop their voices* at the end of a sentence. 'We have just been speaking to … *mumble mumble* …'

Actors of the old school know how to project their voices, so you can hear every word they speak – Judi Dench can whisper and you can still hear her at the back of the circle. But modern actors have been deliberately taught to mumble (it seems to us) because it's more 'naturalistic'.

As a young reporter, I once had to telephone an elderly actress, very famous in her day, called Gladys Cooper. When I addressed her a little nervously over the phone, she barked: 'Speak up, gel! Don't mumble!' I get it now.

Some voices are clearer than others and some accents easier than others. I find the best diction often comes from Scottish voices. Listen to Nicola Sturgeon and hear every crisp word she utters.

Hearing loss is becoming more common among a generation who listened to a lot of loud rock music in their youth. This means that there will be more research and improvements in aids for the deaf. And it's pleasing to see so many public events now accompanied by sign language – a beautiful form of mime reminiscent of ballet movements.

It's understandable that Cilla felt depressed about her impending deafness. Yet it's a condition that can often be greatly helped and supported.

St Anthony – Patron Saint of the Absent-Minded

13 June

'Being old' – a colleague senior to me by some decades once told me – 'means spending most of the day looking for lost property. Glasses, keys, a book I just put down, tickets for a concert, notes, pens, everything.' I have always been mildly absent-minded, so it didn't bother me. I clearly remember leaving an item I had just purchased in a shop when I was twenty (and in Paris), and I have done that at regular intervals over the years.

And then there's the familiar ritual, which I think nearly everyone has experienced, of going upstairs to fetch something and then, when entering the room where that something reposes, experiencing a complete blank about the purpose of your search.

St Anthony, the saint with a reputation for finding objects, thus has a very wide following: even those who are not inclined to faith occasionally call on St Ant to locate lost items.

I was once in Warsaw with a group which included an elderly actor who had lost his return plane ticket to London, as well as his passport. For my part, I had lost a camera on a train from Vilnius to the Polish capital. We set off to find a nearby church with a statue of St Anthony, and when I found it, I think I put ten US dollars in the saint's collection box. It's a good cause, and anyway, I support distributism – G. K. Chesterton's economic belief in spreading money around.

Within half a day, the plane ticket, passport and camera had all turned up. The camera had been handed in, voluntarily, to the railway lost-property office.

Rationalists may claim these things are just coincidences. Psychologists may say that beseeching St Anthony takes your mind off the anxiety about the lost object, and relaxation may help the unconscious mind to locate where something was last placed.

There is also the position of acceptance: some things will be lost and never found. St Anthony may be telling you to resign yourself to that and move on.

But I've learned something about the avoidance of losing stuff. Try to keep possessions in their allotted place and try not to change that allotted place. If your spare keys are kept in a biscuit tin behind the kitchen clock, don't, without very good cause, alter that arrangement. The place where the item is kept is 'fixed' somehow within your neural system, and once that place is changed, you'll spend days desperately searching for it.

'A place for everything and everything in its place' may sound like banal good housekeeping, but it is the central rule of keeping archives. If you can't find an important document, you might as well not have it. Unless you make an especially efficacious plea to St Ant.

Father's Day

20 June

My father died on Father's Day – 20 June – although I don't think that date had been designated as such in the year that he departed this world, 1949. I was five and my memory of him is quite slight, though probably reinforced by stories from my siblings, by family lore and by photographs. Many people have lost a parent in early life: it's striking how frequently this occurred in times gone by, especially when TB ravaged the life of young adults. The Brontë children lost their mother before she was forty, and they were all just young children. But my father was old – he was sixty-seven when I was born – so he had lived a full enough life.

People have managed quite well with one parent, or even with no parents – thrown, as orphans, upon the world. I was cherished by other members of my family, and yet I grew up feeling a rueful kind of envy of children who had both a mother and a father, which seemed to be the norm back in the 1950s. Little girls who talked about 'my daddy' were, I thought, exceptionally lucky. Later on, I grew to realise that not every father is a good father, and I encountered more than a few women – particularly, I think, in the feminist movement – who considered their fathers cruel, oppressive, negative, cold, distant and generally inadequate.

I formed the opinion that women who have trouble with men often had trouble with their fathers – not long ago, a woman I know said it to me: 'I've come to the conclusion I'm not very good at relationships. And I think it's because I didn't get on with my father.'

Perhaps because I didn't have a living father, I came to idealise the role of the good father. To have a good father is a wonderful thing in life, and it strikes me as painful when parents split up and children have less day-to-day contact with their father. Another friend of mine whose father, similarly, died when she was very young told me that whatever difficulties she might encounter in her marriage, she would never, ever 'rock the boat' and risk a divorce – she would never want her own children to be parted from their father.

I probably over-idealise my late father still, and every 20 June I honour his memory.

Merry Widow or Forlorn Spouse?

23 June

It's very worthy of the United Nations to designate 23 June International Widows' Day. Widows have often had a difficult life, as in so many societies widowhood was associated not just with loss of a spouse, but also loss of a breadwinner. The 'poor widow' features in the New Testament as providing her small mite's contribution; in Viennese opera, by contrast, we sing along with *The Merry Widow*.

In his memoir of Ireland in the 1940s, Tim Pat Coogan writes poignantly about his mother's long struggle to obtain a widow's pension after his father died; even though his father had an important government job, as Commissioner of Police, widows and their pensions were often neglected. My own mother became an impoverished widow, and I observed, too, a sometimes worrying decrease in financial security once I was widowed myself. However, as I claimed the right to financial independence as a young feminist, I can hardly complain that, as a widow, I must now put that financial independence into practice.

Widows have been lonely; they have felt deprived of sexual fulfilment; they have been enjoined to dress in black in many Latin cultures. At the Somme museum in Peronne, there is an effigy of a war widow, circa 1916, shrouded in a black veil. In journalism, a lone word at the end of a paragraph was called a 'widow': something left over which could become a problem of spacing. In India, traditionally, a widow was expected to throw herself on the funeral pyre of her husband: this was known as 'suttee', and one of the many enlightened measures of the British Raj was to stop this self-immolating tradition which assumed that women had no lives of their own.

After a period of mourning – once designated at a year and a day – some widows have found that they felt liberated to be themselves. My mother-in-law experienced a sense of being herself, at last, after growing accustomed to widowhood: she was of a generation of women who felt dominated, first by fathers and then by husbands, though formidably intelligent and full of character herself. But it doesn't happen to everyone. It often surprises me that many modern women, while affirming autonomy, still feel lost when their life partner dies.

In *The Playboy of the Western World*, the Widow Quin is seen as somewhat racy and bold. She too had her real-life counterparts.

St Benedict's Rule for Business-Folk

11 July

We don't know an awful lot about St Benedict, who died about 547 AD at Monte Cassino in Italy (now more associated with a famous battle in the Second World War). But, interestingly, his legacy endures, not only among monks and other religious communities – Benedict is considered to be the father of Western monasticism – but also among business leaders. Kit Dollard is one of the co-authors of a book called *Doing Business with Benedict*, which applies the Benedictine rules to the running of a business (most people, apparently, think the Benedictine rules come from Harvard Business School rather than deriving from something penned in the sixth century).

But Benedict was running a community, and a community is not unlike a business or a workplace. You have to have consideration for everyone. You have to have leadership but, at the same time, collegiality. You do have to have a leader (the abbot), but if the group gets too big, then you need to split the community into sections – Benedict would appoint various priors to lead the sections, whereas the business-folk call these priors 'team leaders'. Benedict emphasised moderation, decent food and drink (he allowed wine, and later beer, in the monasteries, but in moderation) and also humility. One of his rules was that the leaders should always listen to the youngest monk, and senior business leaders are enjoined to listen to the newest person who has joined the company. Indeed, listening to everyone is a key part of the Rule of Benedict.

Sometimes, Benedict realised, you have to be stern: if someone is behaving badly and upsetting the rest of the group, they have to go. In his day, they would be excommunicated from the monastery; today, they may have to be fired – every boss has faced that possibility.

Advice from Benedict has survived over the past fifteen hundred years: 'Give the strong something to strive after; show the weak they have nothing to run from.' 'A good word is better than the best gift.' Modern mindfulness, which is recommended for depression and stress, owes quite a lot to the monastic traditions of Benedict's rule. Benedict founded his monasteries to serve God – and the common good – but business leaders today who are searching for ethical guidelines often find Benedict's ideas enrichening.

The Glamour of Crime

Sometimes you learn more about a social problem from a work of fiction than from a fact-based report. Psychologically, a movie or a novel can often illuminate a situation vividly.

The film *Goodfellas* explained, to me, more about the attractions of crime for some youngsters than any amount of sociological studies. When life is tough, even drab, life as a big shot in the crime world can seem incredibly glamorous.

This was also well articulated by a listener to the *Ryan Tubridy Show* on RTÉ Radio 1 who sent an email about her experiences in inner-city Dublin: 'When small-time community drug-dealers show off their fast cars, their three-month holiday photos on Facebook and their fancy clothing, it creates admiration among youths; they aspire to be like the drug dealer, to get to the top and to be the new kingpin,' she wrote.

Exactly so.

The truth is that crime can often seem an attractive career choice. After a lifetime's experience as a barrister, always defending rather than prosecuting, the late John Mortimer (author of *Rumpole*) said that the most frequent reason for a young man turning to crime was 'excitement'. 'Even being a burglar is tremendously exciting,' he said.

I am sure that there are many social problems contributing to crime. Those who are concerned with prison and prison reform report that the majority of offenders have had, to say the least, pretty bad luck in life. Many have never been taught to read and write. A friend of mine who taught literacy in a Kentish prison said: 'Most of the men that I encounter have never really been loved.' A high percentage of prison offenders also have mental health problems.

Many factors feed into the mix. But a life of crime can still seem exciting – as we know from every TV thriller we watch. When I was hooked on *Breaking Bad*, I really wanted Walter White, cooking up drugs for wicked Mexican cartels, to emerge victorious.

The Best Sermon I Ever Heard

One summer evening a certain priest was travelling from the south of England to Liverpool. This was in the 1990s and before the era of the ubiquitous mobile phone. It's a long way from Kent to Merseyside, and about twenty miles before he reached his destination, Father Eamon observed with dismay that he was running out of petrol. The car shuddered to a halt as he pulled into a lay-by, and he pulled into a lay-by on the motorway.

He decided to try and flag down a passing motorist for assistance, but he stood there for twenty minutes while vehicle after vehicle flashed by, ignoring him. Nobody came to his aid. He wasn't wearing clerical clothes: he just looked like an ordinary guy stranded at a lay-by.

The sun was setting and it was getting late. He began to calculate how long it would take him to walk to the next petrol station or roadside telephone box.

Then, out of nowhere, a phalanx of Hell's Angels suddenly drew up, skidding to a halt on their big, noisy Harley-Davidsons. *Oh, jakers*, thought Eamon, *I'll be robbed blind by this lot*, noting their wild hair, metal-studded jackets and multiple body piercings.

They asked if he was in trouble, and he explained that he had been foolish enough to allow the petrol tank to go dry. 'We'll see you all right,' they told him and they sped off.

He sat in his car wondering what would happen next.

Within a short time the bikers were back again with a full can of petrol, which they poured into his tank. They had also purchased water and soft drinks in case the stranded traveller was thirsty.

Refreshed and re-petrolled, the cleric was then accompanied by the Hell's Angels bikers into the centre of Liverpool in convoy, providing him with an escort until he reached his destination. The bikers wouldn't accept any money for the cost of the petrol or the drinks. They were glad to be of help to someone stranded on the road, they said.

'And that,' Father Eamon concluded, when he recounted the experience in a homily, 'is the story of the Good Samaritan.' It can be the most unexpected person who helps you out when you're in a tight corner. Don't judge by appearances.

Why Jane Austen Still Matters

How interesting the enduring appeal of Jane Austen. She writes about the very closed little world of the English gentry in the early nineteenth century, and if her style is admirable, her range is limited. She never describes conversations between men (because, evidently, she was never in the room when men spoke without the presence of women). For her, servants are invisible and we never hear of them, though her characters must, surely, have been looked after by servants – even a modest household required maids in the days before the vacuum cleaner and the washing machine.

Her characters are notably locked within their own class, and they are often prey to petty snobberies, although, admittedly, Jane handles their snobberies with a rapier irony. The great events of the outside world – the wars, the colonialism, the political upheavals, the industrial revolution – seldom get a mention, except where a posting serves to facilitate a character's entrances or exits.

Yet Jane Austen's reach is universal and her work eternal because she is writing about one of the most important subjects in any individual's life and in the life of a family: whom a person might marry; which characters will enter their lives through matrimonial arrangement; who will form that dynastic union which may assure (or promise) the continuation of a family, its genes and its inheritance?

Whom you marry, or whom your offspring marry, is, quite literally, the be-all and the end-all of your life's narrative (significant, too, whom you do not marry). Your spouse will shape, or influence, the course of your life and will contribute to, if not altogether determine, the character and destiny of your children. A woman of good character can be the key and the spur to a man's life and career; a man of solid support can be the whole context for a woman's success. A bad or unsuitable spouse can be – or can contribute to – the ruination of an individual. The character and personality of children will depend upon that essential chemistry between nature and nurture, and the genes they draw upon will be of the essence.

In our day and age, when a marriage can be dissolved and an erroneous match can be unmade by a divorce, we might imagine that spouse-choosing matters much less. And yet, as any mother or grandmother will attest, that choice seems to be as important as ever. Miss Austen endures for a very good reason.

By Virtue of Habit

Sometimes I'll go to church at a weekend and ask myself, 'Am I just going through the motions? Am I a fraud and an imposter, sitting here in a church pew and feeling generally dreary and far from spiritual in any way?' Faith becomes meaningless when it is just an empty ritual, a community habit – when it is just routine, without any commitment of the heart.

There are other times, too, when I feel I'm just 'going through the motions'. Many writers have this experience when they sit down to write. Mark Haddon, author of that compelling story *The Curious Incident of the Dog in the Night-Time*, has said that he will sometimes sit down to put words on a screen knowing that he will delete half of what he has written – perhaps all of it, on some days. He's just going through the motions of writing.

Sometimes you have to cling on to the sheer procedure of habit. Habit, and technique too, can get an actor through a stage performance when he feels in no mood to go on. Body and soul feel devoid of inspiration: it's just 'muscle memory' – the body is merely going through its paces because the body has been trained in a procedure. Even when people have dementia, if they have played tennis all their lives, they can still play tennis because the 'muscle memory' of the body has mastered the process.

Even without any joy, desire or feeling, I tell myself, 'Do what you need to do, just mechanically.' Put one foot in front of the other and continue with the form. Sit in the pew feeling a total spiritual emptiness. Go to the computer screen, utterly devoid of energy or inspiration. Do the piano practice when you least feel like it.

There may come a day, in the long run, when you finally feel that there is no purpose, there are no rewards, in continuing to do something from which meaning and affection have drained away. A couple may keep up a rocky marriage for the sake of form, for the family, in the hopes that it will get back on track. Sometimes it just doesn't. So be it. Yet even when a commitment at a deep level lingers or remains, there are times when you feel you are just leadenly going through the motions. Keep doing it. Fake it till you make it. Often, in the end, you do.

Journalism Day

25 June

I read of a woman who had taken up journalism at the age of seventy-eight and almost instantly made a great success of it. It sort of happened by accident and she made it sound as though it all came naturally and was very easy: someone asked her to write a regular column, and it was greeted with acclaim. About this, I have to admit to mixed feelings. Generally, I cheer when I learn of someone accomplishing something in old age – or even starting something in their sixties or seventies. That Cervantes wrote *Don Quixote* at the age of sixty-seven is nothing less than inspirational.

But somewhere in the reptile part of my brain – that primitive and not very noble element of the inner, shameful self – I don't like to be told that it is easy to fall into a trade like journalism and make a success of it, all quite seamlessly, at any age. Some of us have sacrificed our lives to the hack trade, trying all the while not to be, exactly, hacks (a hack is someone who will write anything for money or on demand: we have most of us come near to it, at times, but we try to tell ourselves such falls from grace are the exception and, really, we try to stay principled). We've fought our way through the thicket of the trade: given up parts of our personal lives we should never have sacrificed, drunk ourselves into an alcoholic stupor, smoked ourselves into a bronchial disaster, slept with catastrophic partners and, probably, prostituted a modest writing talent which might have been developed into something better by churning out, relentlessly, for the deadline. We've lived for the deadline and paid the price of whatever small achievements we have attained in our careers.

And then someone comes along and just glides into journalistic success, finding it all delightfully easy and all doors are opened to her. It's too provoking.

When my brother James was dying, I left his side to fulfil a journalistic assignment. I can hardly bear to think of what I did and the utter wrongness of my priorities when I put journalism before all other considerations. I have had the modest success of remaining in work for over fifty years, but the price is sometimes too painful to think about.

Peter and Paul

29 June

The feast of St Peter and Paul falls on 29 June. The duo, besides being saints, are two of the most fascinating characters in the New Testament.

It is sometimes said that Peter is the Catholic saint – the simple fisherman, sometimes weak and flawed, and yet the first pope, who was martyred for his faith and became the rock on which the church was built; while Paul is the Protestant saint – the inspirational preacher, the wordsmith who contributed some of the most dazzling passages to scripture, and to language. Latterly, Paul has been blamed for misogyny – since he thought women should obey their husbands and he was a bit tough on same-sex relationships – but he was a Hellenised Jew drawing on the classical world, and the context of his culture has to be understood.

Peter is a lovable, human character who is the foundation of the Catholic faith: that mosaic inscription in the Vatican which reads '*Tu es Petrus et super hanc petram Aedificabo Ecclesiam Meam*' is somehow moving. It goes back such a long time.

Yet Paul evangelised brilliantly, underlining Christianity's universality, open to all. And any writer must admire the way he crafted words:

Though I speak with the tongues of men and of angels, and have not charity, I am become as sounding brass, or a tinkling cymbal ... Charity suffereth long and is kind: charity envieth not; charity vaunteth not itself, is not puffed up ... When I was a child, I spoke as a child, I understood as a child, I thought as a child; but when I became a man, I put away childish things. For now, we see through a glass, darkly; but then face to face: now I know in part; but then shall I know even as also I am known. And now abideth faith, hope, charity, these three; but the greatest of these is charity.

When I read Paul's First Letter to the Corinthians, Chapter 13, this, I know, is the divine in prose.

Talking to the Wall

A reporter observed an old man praying at the Jerusalem Wall and noted that he had been there for some time. The journalist went over to the old chap and asked if he might ask him how long had he had been praying at the wall.

'Twenty years,' replied the gentleman. 'Every day for twenty years.'

'And may I ask,' continued the reporter, 'what you have been praying for?'

'Over that time, I have been praying for peace,' replied the venerable.

The journalist proceeded to the clichéd question. 'And after twenty years, how do you feel about your mission?'

'I feel,' said the old man, 'that I might as well be talking to the wall.'

America's Day

4 July

America is often disparaged for its awful gun laws, its increasing inequalities, its imperialist reach and its worship of the almighty dollar, but it's a great country which has brought awesome benefits, joy and uplift to humankind.

For the Fourth of July, let's list some of the great things about America.

- America seldom failed to come to the aid of destitute Irish people in the decades after the Great Famine of the 1840s.
- The West of Ireland, in particular, would have starved, even in the twentieth century, without remittances from exiles who had the opportunity to earn money in America.
- Life, liberty and the pursuit of happiness may not always be attainable, but it's an inspiring aspiration.
- Freedom of expression is a quintessentially American idea and we should stand by it.
- The dream factory of Hollywood made dark childhoods brighter, brought a thankful escape to hard lives and hard times and furnished glamour, drama, narrative and beautiful costumes to an awed world.

- Let's not forget the western, built on fables that the whole world understands: heroes and villains, wars over land, feuds over territory, crime and punishment and, above all, Marlene Dietrich as the saloon keeper in *Destry Rides Again* (with her fabulous chanson: 'Go see what the boys in the backroom will have / And tell them I'm having the same ...').
- The essence of an American film is nearly always – with a few bleak exceptions – that there can always be redemption. That's a great American ideal to hold on to.
- Country and western music. Big bands. Jazz. Gospel. Cole Porter, Irving Berlin, Jerome Kern, Rodgers and Hammerstein, and all the rest. Never forgetting Sinatra, Crosby and Ella Fitzgerald.
- Or Fred Astaire and Ginger Rodgers.
- Woody Allen. Ernest Hemingway. Louisa May Alcott. John Updike. Tennessee Williams. Arthur Miller. Raymond Chandler.
- *Breaking Bad. Madmen. Homeland.*
- The washing machine: few things have liberated women more than the washing machine, invented by an American engineer in 1908.
- Silicon Valley and all the amazing innovations that have emerged from it.
- The patronage of the arts and the endowments of libraries that rich American philanthropists have always upheld. Go to a theatre in New York and count the number of donors at the back of the theatre programme.
- Andrew Carnegie, who said, 'to die rich is to die disgraced'.
- The pursuit, not just of life, liberty and happiness, but also optimism.

Forgiveness – A Tough Call

Christian ideals are pretty hard to reach, and small wonder that few of us measure up to some of the aspirations of the ideal.

Malcolm Muggeridge once said of the Ten Commandments – our Jewish heritage, after all – that he always thought of them as being like an exam paper: 'Seven questions only to be attempted.'

From the New Testament itself, I think one of the toughest exercises that has ever been put to human nature is 'Turn the other cheek.' The beautifully phrased passage from the authorised version says: 'Whosoever shall smite thee on thy right cheek, turn to him the other also.' (It goes on to advise against litigation: 'And if any man will sue thee at the law, and take away thy coat, let him have thy cloke also.')

Really, this is asking way too much of poor, frail human flesh!

The problem with 'turning the other cheek' – never taking revenge for a slight, an offence or an insult – is that it is a completely unnatural reflex. Our nature tells us to strike back. We sometimes even call it 'deterrence'.

And no one wants to be taken for a doormat. When someone hurts your feelings – indeed, is truly mean and malicious towards you – your instinct tells you that she's 'walking all over you' if you don't respond in like manner.

But: resist. Walk away. Make your case in a civilised tone and with respect. Resist the urge to hit back.

Have I always followed this path of wisdom? No, I have not. But I know that I should.

In politics or international affairs, an excess of 'turning the other cheek' can be called appeasement. Yet appeasement springs from fear of a tyrant, rather than an aspiration towards forbearance and charity.

And, as Hilaire Belloc demonstrated in a witty couplet, absolute pacifism may yield to a bully's victory:

Pale Ebenezer thought it wrong to fight,
But Roaring Bill (who killed him) thought it right.

A tough call, turning the other cheek.

Bastille Day

14 July

I wouldn't want to seem in any way disrespectful to the traditions of the French people, but each time that Bastille Day comes around, marking the beginning of the French Revolution in 1789, I increasingly reflect on Daniel O'Connell's experiences during that time and how wise his conclusions were.

O'Connell was just a schoolboy studying at Douai in France, and he spent some time in the small nearby town of St Omer – I know it well, for it is twinned with Deal, where I live. He never forgot what he saw during that period after the Revolution, known as the Terror, when blood ran in the streets and severed heads were displayed on pikes.

It gave him a lifelong revulsion against political violence. But it also developed in his mind a commitment to social and political change through the rule of law and parliamentary accountability. The rule of law, not violence in the streets or violence through any other means, was, for Daniel O'Connell, the motor which would bring change: political emancipation which he championed, initially for Catholics, who were disadvantaged in the United Kingdom at that time, then for Jews, who similarly had restrictions on entering parliament, and then, acting as an exemplar and a mentor to Frederick Douglass in America, for African Americans – the Great Dan was also a supporter of the anti-slavery cause.

O'Connell had sympathy for Wolfe Tone's fiery Irish patriotism, but he did not go along with Tone's support for the French Revolution because he retained that horror of blood in the streets. O'Connell stuck to his principle: peaceful change through the rule of law and, eventually, through parliamentary democracy.

In today's violent world, where there is so much tragic and distressing bloodshed arising from terrorism, O'Connell's message seems more important than ever. There may be, as the Book of Ecclesiastes says, 'a time for war' – if a nation is under attack, it must defend itself – but surely politics, wherever possible, should proceed through the parliamentary process and the rule of law?

For most French people today, 14 July is just a national holiday and is hardly political at all – the details of the French Revolution, as witnessed by Daniel O'Connell, have been lost in the mists of time. It has been a harmless occasion for jollity and celebrations – alas, more recently tainted with the memory of the heinous atrocity against innocent families in Nice, on the French Riviera, in 2016.

But 14 July is also, to me, a reaffirmation that O'Connell's peaceful, legal and constitutional path was the right one, and the one that should be a shining example to the world.

To Thine Own Self Be True?

As schoolgirls, we used to keep autograph books in which we would write little messages as mementoes of friendship. Two much-cited quotes came from Shakespeare: one was 'to thine own self be true, / And it must follow, as the night the day, / Thou canst not then be false to any man.' The other was 'Those friends thou hast, and their adoption tried, / Grapple them unto thy soul with hoops of steel.' The archaic language didn't mean a lot to us, but the quotes always sounded high-minded.

This advice comes from a character regarded as the greatest bore ever created by Shakespeare – Polonius, the father of Ophelia and Laertes, a prize windbag who is given to handing out platitudes. So we're not sure whether Shakespeare means the counsel to be taken sincerely or whether he's mocking tedious old blabbermouths who utter blinding flashes of the obvious. Incidentally, Polonius's most famous lines – 'neither a borrower nor a lender be' – would cause modern banking and global capitalism to grind to a halt, since lending and borrowing is what makes money go around. (Some suggest that might be no bad thing.)

So is 'to thine own self be true' to be taken seriously or dismissed as claptrap? I suppose it does evoke the question: 'What is my true self?' More than fifty years on from those schoolgirl autograph books, I can sincerely answer that I haven't a clue. In a general sense, I suppose we should aim to be sincere and 'genuine'; but personally, my own true self is so compromised by life's turbulent struggles for survival that I don't think I could find it with a radar probe. When Glen Campbell sang in 'Rhinestone Cowboy' 'there's been a load of compromisin' / on the road to my horizon', I thought, yes, that's the true self. A load of compromising.

And yet Polonius was absolutely on the money about friendship and the counsel to grapple steel-like those pals who have proved constant. A good friend who retains friendship through all the difficulties, who doesn't fall out with you and go off on 'non-speakers' because of a misunderstanding, who doesn't feud and quarrel, who sees the big picture and how valuable are shared memories, whose adoption has been tried through thick and thin – oh, yes, grapple, grapple, grapple.

The Madeleine

22 July

France – that society so famous for its secularism – has always celebrated 22 July as the feast of St Mary Magdalene, sometimes known as Mary of Magdala. She is an attractive figure in the New Testament, evidently a follower of Jesus – very often depicted in biblical-based paintings – and, it is implied, a repentant prostitute.

Some of the loveliest churches are dedicated to Mary Magdalene, including the stunning Madeleine church in Paris, facing the boulevard of the Rue de Rivoli and not far from Place de la Concorde. It has always been a fashionable church – so near to the shopping area and so convenient for Maxim's, the famous restaurant. When the fashion designer Coco Chanel died in 1971, her funeral was held at La Madeleine in a requiem Mass (Chanel was surprisingly devout, in her own particular way, with a special devotion to St Thérèse of Lisieux), and Chanel's fashion models carried her coffin on their shoulders, no doubt as if the aisle were a catwalk.

There is a literary attachment, too, to the Madeleine: a madeleine is a little sponge cake (Americans might even call it a cookie) which Marcel Proust dipped into his tea and which instantly provided the total recall of childhood – the remembrance of things past that brought forth his great literary work. This cake was first produced in 1845 by a French cook bearing the name of Madeleine Paulmier, who gave Proust's madeleine her own baptismal name.

There's also an expression in French, 'to weep like a Madeleine' (*pleurer comme une Madeleine*), which refers to the tears with which Mary Magdalene washed the feet of Jesus. The origin of this expression is traced to Balzac, so there's another literary link.

Homes for 'fallen women', and, subsequently, simply young girls who had babies out of wedlock (and were frequently disowned by their families), were also named after Magdalene – first introduced to society by Scottish Calvinists and later copied by Catholics in Ireland. The idea, originally, was compassionate (as was the original idea for orphanages) but they came to be associated with enforced laundry labour and cruelty.

A beautiful name, Madeleine, and in 2016, for the first time in Christian history, her memorial day, 22 July, was made an official feast of the church.

The Meaning of Empiricism

I have recently learned that I am an empiricist, because I have only recently learned what 'empiricist' means. It means someone who judges by experience, rather than theory.

The more experience that I garner, the more I endow it with retrospective judgement. That's empiricism.

Experience is often a terrific guide. One reason why doctors (and often judges, if they don't get too lofty and out of touch) give better professional value when they are older is because they have the experience. They have had most ills, aches, pains and maladies presented to them – and if, by any chance, you have an unusual complaint, they'll be all the more fascinated, since nothing excites a physician more than an unusual case. And so it's an opportunity for them to accumulate more experience.

Almost anything you have done previously becomes a little easier with repetition, and you grow a little more skilful in handling it. Even something you don't do naturally very well, you can still do better with experience.

But you can always draw the wrong lesson from experience. The generals conducting the First World War drew on their experience of previous wars, which, with the technical innovations of 1914 – such as the invention, and terrifying employment, of mustard gas and barbed wire on which soldiers hung and died – made their experience uselessly outdated. A cavalry charge is seldom applicable in the age of tanks.

I much identify with a witty poem that Wendy Cope wrote about a young woman kept choosing the wrong men, and learned never to make the same mistake again – only to make a new mistake instead.

There's the voice of experience: you learn not to make the mistake that you made before. You make an entirely fresh one in its place. And so your pool of empirical experience grows ever greater ...

All Do Not Get Prizes

Many years ago I encountered an American singer visiting London. She was a pleasant woman with a lovely, clear soprano voice, but she wasn't widely known because her speciality was 'ghosting' the voices of actresses who were not professional singers.

Her name was Marni Nixon, and she had been dubbed 'the ghostess with the mostest'. Marni was the singing voice of Deborah Kerr in *The King and I* in 1956, faultlessly matching Miss Kerr's precise, very English speech register. Then she went on to sing the high notes for Natalie Wood in *West Side Story* in 1961 and took over the singing parts for Audrey Hepburn in the film version of *My Fair Lady* in 1964.

But the big studios tried to keep Marni Nixon a secret, and even threatened that she'd never work again if she disclosed the fact that she was the voice behind the stars. (The stars themselves reacted differently, incidentally: Deborah Kerr, who was unassuming and hard-working, fully acknowledged Miss Nixon's gifts; Natalie Wood, who had been a child star and was apt to be spoiled, was furious that Marni should assist her. I met both of these film stars: loved Miss Kerr's simplicity and sincerity; loved Miss Wood's exquisitely cut ocelot fur coat.)

By 1966, it was gradually leaking that Marni had contributed to the success of these terrific musicals, but she was never really awarded the honours – or the royalties – that she merited. She was certainly never accorded the billing, which is a major issue in the performance arts: the movie posters of *West Side Story* and *My Fair Lady* should, in justice, have carried the coda that Marni Nixon provided the best of the female voice parts.

When she died at age eighty-six in 2016, her talent and contribution were finally widely recognised in obituaries; still, during her lifetime Hollywood never paid her the tributes she deserved.

The moral of the story is that the people who deserve honours don't always get them. And people who may have done little except please a powerful politician, been fortunate in their connections – or even, perhaps, schmoozed with the key individuals at the right moment – may be showered with the glittering prizes. The best arbiter of prizes and awards is history, although even then, as Thomas Gray noted in his elegy, many a flower is born to blush unseen.

The Pitfalls of Advice

My mother's advice on the eve of my marriage was: 'Never let the sun go down on your anger' and 'Never give a man bad news on an empty stomach.' Her words were both wise and witty, and I have often reflected upon them. The difference between my mother's generation and mine is that, while they thought it a duty to pass on advice to a younger generation, amazingly, they even thought older people should be respected! In our generation, we're addressed as equals – thanks for that! – and we are excoriated if we ever dare to suggest the smallest counsel. We are strictly prohibited from handing out advice to the young. In the first place, they'd rebuff it. In the second place, they'd say, 'Don't you dare tell me how to live my life!' In the third place, they'd say we hadn't the faintest clue about anything. So, like the old man praying in Jerusalem, you might as well be talking to the wall.

Yet another phrase Ma used to utter (and I have heard it from other daughters recalling a mother's words): 'You'll learn!' Oh, yes. Eventually. It will take many years and a lot of bad choices, but eventually, yes.

If I were to give advice to a younger generation, however, I would just say: 'You live in a vale of tears. Get used to it.' That life is a valley of tears may be a cause for weeping but not a reason to despair. A dismaying number of people in Winston Churchill's life took their own lives – he lost a brother-in-law, a former stepfather, a former daughter-in-law, a son-in-law and a daughter to suicide – but despite his 'black dog' depressions he remained opposed to it, because, he said, you miss out on 'what happens next'. His rule of life was to 'keep buggering on'.

Grit is the most important component in all endeavours and tenacity the most vital element in character. You're in the valley of tears, so (to mix the metaphors) find some lemons and make lemonade.*

*'If life gives you lemons, make lemonade!'

Four Literary Masters

It is said that the four great masters of the modernist novel are Marcel Proust, James Joyce, Italo Svevo and Franz Kafka. How interesting that three of the four were Jewish and one Catholic (at least by formation).

Actually, although his mother came from a distinguished Jewish family – the mother being the key to Jewish identity – Marcel Proust was raised and confirmed as a Catholic. He never practised the Catholic faith, but he deplored the French political secularism which, he felt, removed such an essential element of beauty from the conduct of life. He thought churches were beautiful and necessary, even if he didn't frequent them.

Joyce gave up his faith, and yet his Jesuit education permeated his work throughout his life: he simply couldn't have been the writer he became without that Catholic education.

Italo Svevo became a close friend of Joyce's when they were both in Trieste (Stanley Price has written a fine study of their friendship), and it is suggested by the author that Svevo became a model for the central character in Joyce's *Ulysses*, the Jewish Dubliner Leopold Bloom, creating an intertwining of these identities.

Kafka is a secular writer, and yet his biographers have discerned a deep awareness of Jewish spirituality in the subtext of his work – as well as a deep awareness of feeling 'different' (which surely any writer should feel).

Writers may discard faith – but they are often richer for drawing on its rich wells of heritage, feeling, culture and purpose.

A Poetry Memorial

It was agreed that I should provide a memorial card for my elder brother Carlos after he died in 2010: his widow, Louise, had a bit rather too much to cope with and so it was my responsibility. Memorial cards have been traditional in Catholic Ireland for years, and any mother's prayer-book used to be stuffed with them. But everything needs updating and revising, and all the traditional cards seemed a bit too religious for my brother, who was an observant Catholic but not exactly holy. His intelligent wife – who died more than five years later – used to joke that Carlos was a 'superstitious' Catholic: he warmed to all the old tales, stories and legends, rather than being engaged with more up-to-date discourses on faith practice.

As a child, he was frequently consigned to the care of the woman who was then our Dublin housekeeper, Lizzie, who was funny, forthright, respectable and, like so many Dubliners of her vintage – she'd have been born in the 1900s – merrily morbid. One of the outings to which she would take Carlos, as a child, was to view dead sailors in the Ringsend morgue. As a balance, there was also a lively practice of attending the weddings of strangers – again, absolutely legal, since the point of a wedding is that it is a public event and should be seen to be done. This was more in the way of admiring the finery and comparing the guests' general appearance.

Lizzie also brought little Carlos to various 'hauntings', a trek around the Seven Churches on Good Friday and a particular spectacle in St Stephen's Green, where the ghost of a Victorian maid was seen to appear: she had been dismissed from service for attending to her religious duties ('twas said) and fell to her death from a window; each Good Friday the Dubliners would foregather to glimpse her spirit.

These tales and legends stayed with my brother, and he enjoyed recounting them much more than he'd have relished a discussion on the ecclesiology of Vatican II. Lizzie passed on to him a kind of magical realist sense of religion (with an awesome attitude to death, which yet allowed for an element of entertainment in its ceremonies). The moral niceties that were often upheld fiercely at the time didn't seem so important.

Carlos also liked to recount how, as a teenage lad, he and his pals – the hard blades – would attend Mass at Sandymount church on a Sunday morning but always make a point of going outside the church porch for a cigarette during the sermon. Just to show the clergy that these young blades weren't about to be too submissive.

So how to choose a memorial card for this dear brother? With the help of an imaginative, although atheist, printer, we produced what I think was a very nice one, with enough memory and spirituality but not too much of a 'Holy Joe' flavour. As for the verse to be cited, I thought that Walter Savage Landor fitted the bill:

> I strove with none, for none was worth my strife.
> Nature I loved, and next to Nature, Art:
> I warm'd both hands before the fire of Life;
> It sinks, and I am ready to depart.

And so, I think, Carlos was ready to depart – although there isn't a day I don't miss him.

My Dream House

I passed my dream house again the other day. This one-and-a-half-storey home, built right on the seafront, represents to me the perfect, the utterly ideal home. It is a long bungalow shape, but it has half a storey upstairs, because I once examined the interior when it was briefly on the market. The half-storey was a very long, loft-like room which could be used as an extra sleeping room: I imagined, when I explored the dream house, gaggles of young visitors – maybe my children and their friends – bedding down there on high-spirited weekend visits. The house has a garden at each end, protected by high bushes, and its every room is just what a room should be – spacious, accommodating to books and with a peerless view over the sea.

I must have imagined acquiring this perfect house during one of our many house-moves – five times in less than twenty years – but either it was beyond our budget or someone else got there first.

So I never acquired my perfect house. So what? Life is full of unrealised ambitions, and, as the late Lynn Anderson sang, 'I never promised you a rose garden'. Edna O'Brien said to me a few years ago: 'I may not be able to climb Mount Errigal anymore, but I can look at it.' And I can still walk past the perfect house and take pleasure in looking at it.

The Americans are great ones for saying that 'it's never too late to follow your dreams': this, I'm afraid, is not always true. It does become too late to follow many of your dreams in this life, and so you must put your dreams aside and count your blessings instead, or take joy from remembering the dream, or be grateful for the lesser achievements.

A couple of years ago, I applied to Birkbeck College at London University to do an MA in drama – a teenage dream I still entertain. It was somewhat wounding not just to be rejected, but also to be told by the admissions tutor – an Irishwoman, alumnus of Trinity College Dublin – that I was 'academically mediocre'. That was an opportunity to practise humility, though my first reaction was anger and fury. But now I think – so what? Maybe I am 'academically mediocre', but who cares? I'd rather think of what the veteran theatre director Peter Brook says: 'Everyone brings something to the table.'

My husband Richard used to say that once you pass sixty, what you most often experience is disappointment. I now think this was too negative. Yes, naturally, disappointment there must be: as soon as there are aspirations, there are disappointments. But even disappointments bring compensations, interesting reflections and the remembrance of a dream. As for that dream house? The salt air of the sea would surely have entailed high maintenance costs against rust and corrosion!

Grammar Lesson

The French have a reputation for being much more exact about language than native English speakers. As a teenager in France I was given a lesson in how one should wield language as an exact tool, not as a vague cover-all.

'A man comes home early from work one day,' I was told by a French schoolteacher, 'to find his wife in the arms of her lover.

'"Madame," he says, reproachfully. "I am surprised!"

'"No, Monsieur," his wife replies. "*We* are surprised. *You* are astonished!"'

And that, I was informed, was the difference between 'surprise' and 'astonishment'.

I was, indeed, 'astonished' by the lesson, and the laconic tone in which it was narrated.

Proud to Be a Shawlie

The shawl – a traditional Irish form of costume – is a great garment. It can be warm or it can be cool. It can be haute couture or it can be bargain-basement budget. It can be worn by the fashion leaders of the globe, and it is worn by some of the poorest people in the world. It can be exquisitely decorative, as in the tradition of the Kashmir pashminas, from where the shawl originally derives, or it can be a bread-and-butter knitted covering. A cotton shawl can be beachwear and a silk cape can adorn a ballgown.

Glance over old photographs of country Irishwomen in Cork and Kerry and the Aran Islands and they are usually provisioned by a shawl, normally in black.

Shawls were worn before anyone could afford a coat, and there are poignant stories of Connaught women in post-famine times who would share a good shawl for special occasions or for a Sunday Mass. In my Dublin childhood, the market-seller mammies in Moore Street always had a shawl (and an old pram in which to move goods).

The shawl was discreet and practical for the purposes of breastfeeding, in the days before breasting was affirmed as a right to be done openly (and, still, some mothers do prefer a little privacy). The shawl also had – and still has – the advantage of, if not exactly concealing a pregnancy, at least sufficiently covering the bump so that no one was quite sure: especially when it was no one else's business. Mothers who find it harder to lose post-baby weight are also well-served by the enveloping shawl.

The mammies and the grannies of old, who would be welcomed into the snug of a Dublin pub (in the days when a respectable woman wouldn't enter the saloon bar), would sit wrapped in their shawls and presently they would go home, carrying beneath the ubiquitous garment an extra pony of porter in a jug. When it rained, the shawl could cover head as well as body.

I have up to a dozen shawls and wraps, and I love them. I have a gorgeous little shoulder-warmer in wool and another, in musquash fur, purchased from a junk shop for £25 and peerlessly warm; I have longer capes from Jimmy Hourihan, and even a longer emerald cloak from Cleo in Dublin which I'm keeping for the day I have a play performed at the Abbey Theatre (probably never, but a girl must hope). I have ponchos, and half-coat capes, and wraparound shawls that can double as dressing-gowns. Yes, I'm proud indeed to be a shawlie.

When a Tragedy Strikes

Whenever a tragedy was reported in the news – a family drowned, an earthquake burying a village, an awful road accident – my mother would quote the couplet: 'Never morn wore on till eve / But some heart did break.' She always ascribed it to Byron – Byron seemed to be the ultimate in romantic thinking for those born in the nineteenth century, or in the early years of the twentieth, and all the more so since he was seen as transgressive. But in fact, it comes from Tennyson, a less transgressive (he was given the stamp of approval both by Queen Victoria and by the Irish bishops, who probably shared many values with the old queen) but powerfully romantic and rueful bard.

How true it is! Every day some heart will break, and we should give it thought, because the thought is linked with pity and compassion and a shared feeling of humanity. And an understanding that we are all vulnerable to the pure chance that can bring tragedy.

The Green Letter Box

I love the green letter boxes that we have in Ireland and I love the story behind their installation. It was the novelist Anthony Trollope who more or less invented the letter box, and when he accepted a post-office job in Ireland in the 1840s, he brought the letter box with his position. Trollope is associated with both Drumsna in Co. Leitrim (where he was inspired to write his first novel, *The Macdermots of Ballycloran* – the ruin which inspired him still stands) and with Shannonside's Banagher, nearby in Co. Offaly, from where he worked. Ireland meant a lot to Trollope because it freed his imagination and his approach to life – he had felt such a failure in England. He had debts, dire trouble and been involved in trouble at work. Thus did he volunteer for service in the West of Ireland. His salary was to be £100 a year. He later called Ireland 'the first good fortune of my life', and knew that he owed his flowering, as a novelist, a person and eventually a husband and father, to his Irish sojourn.

But Ireland also benefited from Trollope's presence in the letter box and the post-office service that he worked hard to establish. A reliable postal service was a great boon to Irish emigrants and to families at home – for news from abroad and for remittances, safely despatched. My grandmother in Galway wrote to my mother in Dublin every day, posting her letter for the 11.30 collection at, I believe, Woodlawn: the letter would arrive by the 4 p.m. delivery in Ballsbridge, Dublin (this was the 1940s: there were still four deliveries a day).

Communications have moved on, as we all know, but many of us still cherish the post, and the letter box is its emblem. Irish letter boxes represent a great variety of design and are well illustrated by Stephen Ferguson's guide, *The Irish Post Box*, available from An Post. There are letter boxes which still bear the monogram of past British monarchs – in particular Edward VII, during whose short reign more letter boxes were erected than in any other – and there are letter boxes from 1923 installed by the Irish state. They are all fabulous to look at – and to use. Some Irish nationalists would scrape off the monarchical monograms (and some have been removed), but that, surely, would reduce the sense of variety and the story of history that they carry. And after all, since the Royal Mail did actually establish the Irish postal service – in the person of Anthony Trollope – surely it would be a denial of historical truth to airbrush the emblem of their memory?

Blossoming Plum and Cherry

Adelaide Crapsey (1878–1914)

Blossoming plum and cherry,
Flowering apple and quince,
In spring time I was merry
I've learned weeping since,
Bitter weeping since.

Adelaide Crapsey was only thirty-six when she died, in 1914, of tuberculosis. Born in Brooklyn, she lost her sister and her brother also to early deaths, and suffered to see her father, an Episcopalian minister, expelled from the church on a heresy charge. She was a college teacher and an accomplished poet who is credited with establishing a new verse form, the cinquain. In these five lines, and twenty-one words, she expresses quite beautifully the mood of ruefulness prompted by a memory of the blossoms of spring.

Autumn

Poem for an Adopted Child

Anonymous

Not flesh of my flesh
Nor bone of my bone
But still, miraculous,
My own.
Never forget
For a single minute –
You didn't grow under my heart
But in it.

When I quoted this anonymous poem in an article in the *Sunday Telegraph* some years ago, I received a warm and appreciative note from the writer Jilly Cooper, whose children were adopted. She said that it meant so much to her, and she thanked me for publishing it. I think it's a wonderful short poem which expresses, in just twenty-nine words, a profound sense of human attachment. Blood links go deep, but attachment by love, care, altruism and responsibility is also part of the human experience, and such an admirable one.

World Suicide Prevention Day

10 September

Suicide has been viewed differently in different cultures. Famously, the Japanese have regarded some forms of suicide as honourable. Not long ago, a businessman in Japan who was being investigated for possible corrupt practices chose to take his own life rather than face the consequences: this was commended by a leading politician as an honourable choice.

The philosopher Arthur Schopenhauer also thought that the ancient world of Greece and Rome had a much more civilised attitude to suicide than Western Christianity, in which there has traditionally been a prohibition against it, as Hamlet explains so well in his soliloquy: 'the Almighty has fixed his canon 'gainst self-slaughter'. Schopenhauer, who was writing in the 1850s, deplored the fact that Western culture regarded suicide as cowardly and shameful, when in fact it could be a rational surrender of an unbearable life.

But according to the Irish Protestant W. H. Lecky, the great historian of European morality, the ancient world didn't always commend suicide. Pythagoras, he writes, forbade men 'to depart from their guard or station in life without the order of their commander, that is, of God'. Plato 'adopted similar language, though he permitted suicide when the law required it, and also when men had been struck down by intolerable calamity'. Aristotle condemned it as being 'an injury to the state'. In Rome, where suicide 'acquired greater prominence, its lawfulness was by no means accepted as an axiom': patient endurance of suffering was more admired. Virgil was negative about suicide, and Cicero broadly followed the doctrine of Pythagoras. Marcus Aurelius 'wavers' on the subject; Seneca advocated suicide while admitting that others thought it wrong; Caesar and Ovid both thought enduring life was more admirable than suicide. The Stoics were pro-suicide, but Plotinus and Porphyry argued against it.

It seems, perhaps, as though the ancient world was as divided about the subject as the modern world is. And Japan started to change its Samurai approach to suicide in the late 1990s, when psychiatrists began to realise that some people who chose suicide were actually depressed and could benefit from treatment. Until the 1990s, Japan had virtually ignored clinical depression. There were even second thoughts about the boss who chose hara-kiri over facing an enquiry into his possibly corrupt business practices. The cultural differences over suicide continue to be fluid.

Grandparents' Day

11 September

I met a couple on a cruise a few years ago and, over dinner, the talk turned to family. Yes, they were grandparents. But they never saw their grandchildren, no. Why? Shoulder shrugs. Family rifts. A divorce split loyalties. Differences arose. And soon it seemed better to drift apart.

I shared a coffee with a clever and attractive young post-grad in Amsterdam and she mentioned that, while she was close to her mother, her father wasn't in her life any more. She never saw her father's mother either, though she was the only grandchild. I imagined a lonely grandmother wondering how her granddaughter had grown and developed and blossomed – and yet had no contact with her. What a sorrow.

Some grandparents are run ragged looking after their grandchildren, and a study from Trinity College Dublin has indicated that those who spend more than sixty hours a week doing childcare are subject to depression, especially if they are less supported themselves. This is understandable. Nature arranged matters so that human beings usually become parents when they are young and fit – twenty-three is, physically, the best age in life to become a mother – and few people have the same energy in their sixties and seventies.

All the same, most grandparents I have encountered love their grandchildren and consider it a privilege to be able to spend time looking after them.

'Look,' says Barbara, who cared for her grandchildren while her son was in hospital, 'what is better than to be *needed*?' She had spent time nursing in a geriatric ward and had been saddened by encountering old people who seldom saw any family members. 'I'd rather be worked to the bone looking after the grandchildren than to be told "you're surplus to requirements".' She was thankful that she had such a good relationship with her daughter-in-law that she was fully trusted with the childcare.

The TCD study highlights facts about family life and childcare today. But I think the inference that grandparenting can cause depression shouldn't be overstated. Any extreme stress can cause depression, but I would suggest there are far more grandparents who relish the contact with their grandchildren than feel oppressed by it.

And I have known so many grandparents who are sad that they see less of their grandchildren than they'd like to. Emigration is, obviously, one reason. There may be plenty of Skyping, and a much-cherished visit to France, or Australia, or California every now and again, but it's not quite the same as the everyday cuddles and kisses that young grandchildren bestow in regular contact.

Strangely, too, affluence and success can be a reason for grandparents seeing less of their grandchildren. The richer the family, the less the grandparents are needed.

One evening I was reading a bedtime story to my younger granddaughter, Eleanor. The story was about the moon. 'Would you like to go to the moon one day?' I asked. 'Yes,' she said, turning to me with a beatific smile. 'With you, Grandma.' Worth any amount of fatigue.

Autumn and Old Age

The onset of old age is remarkably like the coming of autumn. The leaves begin to fall, there's a bit of a chill in the air by the end of August and the nights draw in. We try to catch at the fading lights of summer and console ourselves that there is still some evening brightness in the air, but we know it is ebbing. The environment becomes a little misty and melancholy, and soon it is time to look back on the year and prepare for year's end.

Time to look back and see where we have gone wrong – oh, so often! 'You'll learn,' my mother used to say. And so I have. Usually the hard way. I sometimes think the purpose of man's biblical lifespan – seventy, being three score years and ten – is that it's just about the time it takes to learn the lessons of life. The joker in the pack being that, like portraying Shakespeare's Juliet, by the time you are mature enough to have authority in the role, you are far too old to play it. You have gained all this knowledge through trial and error, but it's too late to do anything about it – at least in this life. Small wonder people of yore placed so much hope in the hereafter: it could be another chance.

When he was into his seventh decade, I interviewed the writer and poet Clive James for a retrospective on the 1960s. He said that what he most disliked and resented about encroaching old age was the feeling of running out of time. There wouldn't be enough *time* to do all he wanted to do – and especially to write all he wanted to write. A few years later, his health deteriorated dramatically – he developed a lung disease, as well as leukaemia. His personal life also became somewhat complicated, and his marriage nearly broke up – he admitted that it was his fault for misbehaving – so he felt very much alone.

And then he started to write the best poetry of his life: poetry to make us feel, to make us weep, to make us draw in our breath with wonder. Its theme has been what Patrick Pearse once called 'the beauty of the world' as we bid it farewell. Autumn may be a sad metaphor for old age, but it may bring its very own wistful and touching gifts.

Regrets, I've Had a Few
(Especially about Education)

There are many things I would do differently if I had my life over again. And I think I'm not alone in claiming that, if only I had known then what I know now, I'd have made better use of my education. But it's only in retrospect that I actually understand what my education was supposed to be about: I didn't understand any of the context then. I would sit in rapt attention, today, to hear our witheringly sarcastic teacher, Miss Blake, explain coniferous and deciduous trees: I thought it was just a boring old list of stuff when I was thirteen, but now I see it is part of the wonders of the earth and the glories and diversity of nature. I hadn't the slightest idea what geometry, either, was for: not understanding it, I made an effort to learn Euclid off by heart. 'The square of the hypotenuse is equal to the sum of the squares of the other two sides.' Sometimes, walking around a city square, or walking through it, I think about Pythagoras's theorem.

What I didn't have then, but what I have now, is context. For me, only many years later did I come to appreciate the context of knowledge. My cousin, who is an accomplished teacher of English to French adults, has explained to me that some people have inductive reasoning, while others grasp theoretical reasoning. People of inductive reasoning have to see, or be shown, how something is applied: they seldom learn from theory alone. English is such an irregular language that, truly, you have to learn from the example of English speakers how the very loose rules are applied. French, by contrast, is based on a grid of logic, and the French cast of mind is thus often theoretical: French students often ask, first, 'What is the grammatical rule?' rather than 'How does this work in practice?'

I think I also had more than a touch of ADD – attention deficit disorder – as a schoolgirl. At that time, this was called 'being a giddygoat', rather than being subjected to a diagnosis and dosed with Ritalin, a drug which allegedly corrects the giddygoat tendency. Maybe if I had been stuffed with Ritalin I would have done better. But each September, how I'd love to be going back to school and starting all over again.

Jewish Harvest Festival

The Jewish harvest festival of Sukkot – held between late September and late October – seems to me to be particularly beguiling. It is a Feast of Nature or a Feast of Ingathering, and it is supposed to last seven days (or, among the diaspora, eight days). There is a different ritual set aside for each day. The most attractive aspect to me, as an outsider, would be the idea of constructing the 'sukkah', which is supposed to be a temporary or fragile dwelling, usually put up in a garden, and eating and sleeping within. Outdoor sleeping, under the stars, is a fabulous experience – I did it in the desert of Egypt. But as with most Jewish festivals, there is more to it than the actual rite: it symbolises something. We should remember those who have had – and many still who have – nothing but a fragile structure to sleep under. We should identify with those who have been through hardships, those who are homeless and those who are refugees. And yet, there is a harvest to be thankful for, which nature provides every year.

Religious or not religious, we urban-dwellers have often lost touch with the rhythm of life, and indeed the hazards that have often governed the lives of those who went before. Holy days like Sukkot are a meaningful reminder of life's cycle, of nature and of our obligation to be thankful for the blessings we bountifully enjoy.

A Bad Trip with Gender Quotas

Gender quotas are favoured by some feminists – setting aside a certain percentage of jobs or positions for women – but I have a miserable memory of being a beneficiary of such thinking. I was once given a job simply because I was a female and, honestly, it led to one of the unhappiest years of my life.

Scroll back to the 1970s, when the editor of the *London Evening Standard* – one Charles Wintour (father of the now more famous Anna, of *Vogue* renown) – decided it must be time to have a female executive among his ranks. There had been female reporters and columnists in Fleet Street since the 1920s but never a female executive, it seemed.

His gimlet eye alighted on me. He lured me back from a job in Dublin in which I flourished and said I would make history. It was, he said, time that women were promoted more.

He said that female input was needed in the direction of the paper. National budgets, he claimed, were always assessed for the price of beer and never for the price of bread. That was because there weren't enough women at the helm.

If someone invites you to do something difficult, shouldn't you always say yes? And so I said yes to a job that was beyond my capabilities and training. It wasn't the macho editorial conferences that fazed me: it was the wide range of responsibilities, from budget sheets to arguments over the bridge column. The well-liked cookery writer was beginning to suffer from senility (omitting crucial ingredients from a recipe) so she had to be fired – a horrible job, firing anyone – and there were tears and lamentations. There was endless detail, personnel management, future planning and the discipline of four editions a day to cope with.

I just wasn't up to it; I didn't know enough; I didn't have the experience or skills. And as this became evident to those around me – and that the editor was merely protecting me because I was his choice – I lost authority and respect. This was the point where I began drinking more heavily. I'd been an enthusiastic imbiber since my late teens, but now, at twenty-nine, the habit took a dark turn. I drank to mask my problems and boost my non-existent confidence – morning, noon and night. I also threw myself into some disastrous relationships.

And the more I drank, the worse I performed at the job – and the more of an eye-rolling response there was from everyone around. My deputy carried the daily responsibilities – those pesky budget sheets! – and it was common knowledge around the office that he had been unfairly passed over because he was a man and the editor wanted to appoint a woman. I can barely think of that year without feeling a sense of mortification. Finally, I asked to step down, and did so. Everyone breathed a sigh of relief.

I'm all for women getting every opportunity in their careers. But in the final analysis, people must be promoted on merit: because they've fought to get the job. Because if they can't cut it, they'll be miserable and all around will be a shambles. Trust me, tokenism of any kind is the road to ruefulness for all concerned.

The Medicalisation of Melancholy

I have the greatest sympathy for anyone who suffers from mental health problems or from clinical depression, which is surely included in mental health. And those who say the stigma against mental ill-health should be removed and everyone who suffers from depression should be open about it are to be supported and encouraged. I see no reason whatsoever why any mental illness should be stigmatised.

And yet a part of me also regrets the medicalisation of all melancholy; and part of me wonders if it's helpful for young people to be told that every element of unhappiness, regret, grief, despair, sorrow, sadness, mourning, anxiety, isolation, disappointment or rejection is essentially a medical condition. Many aspects of the human condition are now classified as 'trauma' – a medical word for a wound – and many sad, shocking or upsetting reactions to a variety of events are termed 'traumatic'.

I even suspect – and I am not the only one – that the medicalisation of human emotions, which will always include depressing and sorrowful ones, has some of its origins in the pharmaceutical industry, which has an interest in pathologising the human condition. Over three thousand medical or psychiatric academic papers are published annually on the subject of depression and mental illness. In his book, *Manufacturing Depression*, the psychotherapist Gary Greenberg suggests that the profits accruing to the pharmaceutical industry are directly linked with the enormous increase in the diagnoses of depression worldwide. 'To the manufacturers of drugs,' he writes, 'diseases are markets.' Another American shrink, Professor Irving Kirsch, suggests that not only are antidepressant drugs driving this profitable 'market', but also, in many cases, placebos – fake compounds – work just as well as costly pharmaceutical antidepressants.

Depression certainly is an affliction; and where it drives individuals to suicide, it kills. But sadness, sorrow and grief are not always 'depression'. They can be natural reactions to a tragic episode in the course of human life. Schopenhauer says that the only guaranteed aspect of the human condition is that we're bound to be subjected to sadness, disappointment, loss, anxiety and fear. He was a bit of an over-gloomy German (a not inconsiderable category) but he has a point. We should teach young people that there are sad and difficult passages in life, and the answer is not always more Seroxat.

Biography in Topography

One of the things I love about France is the way they name their streets, in every small town and village, after people from their history, literature and culture. You don't see much of 'High Street' and 'Main Street' in the French landscape: almost every town has an Avenue Jean Jaures (the socialist political leader who was assassinated in 1914), perhaps a Rue Victor Hugo, Quai Voltaire, Place Jean Moulin (the Resistance hero who died under torture in 1943) or Centre Pasteur. The writers, the artists, the scientists, the musicians – even those not belonging to France, as in the Avenue Mozart in Paris – are commemorated, as are some kings (the more distant ones, rather less the last monarchs, though poor guillotined Louis XVI probably deserves some retrospective pity) and many saints.

It's rather beguiling that anti-clerical and secularist campaigners such as Jules Ferry and Leon Gambetta often nestle quite cosily with local saints, as well as the peerless St Joan of Arc. In St Omer, there is a very pretty wayside shrine to Our Lady nicely placed in the Rue Gambetta – indeed, the very name of the street is positioned directly over the Madonna statue enclosed in a glass case. This can be seen as a nice metaphor of the way in which disparate, and at one time warring, traditions in a nation can be woven together without anyone quite noticing what is going on.

Naming the streets for people brings history and biography to life, and I don't know why it isn't done more in Britain and Ireland, where biography in book form is a more successful genre than it is in France. There are some locations, yes, that carry a historical allusion: there's always a Waterloo Place and a Wellington Place, an O'Connell Street and a Pearse Street. But it's much less common. Nelson's Pillar in Dublin was, famously, blown up by the IRA in 1966, but for decades there had been dithering about who should be atop the pillar instead of the admiral. Somewhat unimaginative naming of roads is more usual: there are twenty-nine 'Avenue Roads' in the London area alone, a pinnacle of under-imaginative topography.

History is essentially about people, and when we walk our streets it is great to be aware that others have trod these very paths before us.

Should a Judge Swear?

Should a judge swear? There was merriment when a British judge, Patricia Lynch, gave as good as she got when the accused in the dock called her by the rude C-word. She directed it right back to the prisoner himself.

Some felt that My Lords and Ladies on the bench should not habitually descend to the same level of discourse as those charged with an ASBO for common abuse.

Perhaps not. But the prevailing rule about court is that you should never irk or patronise the judge. The old lawyers' joke, which appeared first in that classic text *The Old Munster Circuit*, tells of a judge who, in a petty case of pilfering, tells the defence lawyer: 'You will be aware of the guidelines – *de minimus non curat lex.*' 'Indeed,' replies the clever-clogs advocate, 'in the hills of Connemara, where my client dwells, they speak of little else!'

Realising he is the object of sarcasm, the judge bangs his gavel and doubles the sentence. Never mess with the judge!

De minimus non curat lex, meaning 'the law is not concerned with trifles', was a fine principle. The trouble with the law today is that it often makes too much fuss over trifles: if a child calls another child a derogatory word in the playground, the offender can be arraigned for racist or homophobic abuse, instead of being sensibly corrected. Indeed, Judge Patricia is herself to be investigated for her 'inappropriate' use of language.

Perhaps phrases like *de minimus* should be aired more frequently in court – leave aside the odd four-letter exchange of invective.

The Sadness of the Lonely …

Loneliness is said to afflict old people disproportionately – it's often called 'an epidemic' among the elderly – and that figures.

When we are more confined to our homes, less able to get out and about, less able to travel to meet old friends or to join groups to make new ones, it's obvious that we're more vulnerable to being lonely.

It's not just an outward kind of loneliness, though, as in lack of company. It's the irrational feeling of being an abandoned child. So many of those you have known and loved have died. All those parental figures, all those aunts and uncles and, in my case, all my siblings have departed this world. And many of the friends of my youth are no more. It leaves you with this deserted feeling: why did they go and leave you, just when you need them most?

My sister Ursula died in 2003, but I could do with talking to her now. Now she'd understand so many of my problems, and now, I would have more understanding of hers. We were just growing more close to one another, even becoming more like each other, when she was taken away.

That's where the loneliness comes from. You can make new friends with the passage of time, and I'm grateful that I have made new friends, but it doesn't quite assuage the loneliness so well described by Thomas Moore in 'Oft in the Stilly Night'.

When I remember all
The friends, so link'd together
I've seen around me fall
Like leaves in wintry weather;
I feel like one,
Who treads alone
Some banquet-hall deserted
Whose lights are fled
Whose garlands dead
And all but he departed!

Activities and interests can and do relieve loneliness, and we can keep in touch with friends and family via mobile phones, emails, Skype and even, yes, letters and cards. But we walk upon the shore more alone, all the same, and hear the tide ebb away, with the great whoosh of its melancholy undercurrent.

… And the Consolations of Solitude

Yet I'm also one of those people who enjoys being alone and enjoys doing things alone. One of the aspects of social life that I fear is that I'll feel obliged to please everyone else so much that I won't feel confident about pleasing myself. If I'm arranging a meal with a companion, I'm anxious as to whether the restaurant is the right place and the menu is suitable. I feel I should bend to their choice rather than insist on my own.

Even worse is shopping with someone else: if someone accompanies me to a shop, I feel I have to buy the item that they think best, rather than whatever I choose. I have bought stuff simply because the person I'm with advises me to. I've even borrowed books and CDs from libraries because a complete stranger said, 'Oh, you should choose this one – it's terrific.' And I've complied, rather than offend the other person. This comes from the trait known as 'people-pleasing' – a desire to feel the approval of someone else as a priority.

When we were growing up, in my generation, we were taught to be humble and always to consider the other person first. At my convent school, table manners were so emphasised that we were told: 'If your neighbour at table has to ask for the salt, you have already failed' – that is, your very first thought ought to be your table neighbour's needs.

All this made for considerate young convent girls, but it also pushed one in the direction of people-pleasing. When the Swinging Sixties hit, all heck broke loose. I once asked a friend of mine if she had ever refused to go to bed with a man, and she replied: 'Well, it seems so disobliging, doesn't it?' The epitome of people-pleasing!

That's the joy – and the freedom – of being alone. You don't have to cringingly please anyone else. There was a poem I learned as a child, whose fragments only stay with me, which dwelt on the theme: 'I can think whatever I want to think, I can say whatever I like to say – there's nobody here but me!'

I've heard women say about the pleasures, or at least consolations, of living alone: 'I answer to no one!'

St Francis – A Universal Figure

4 October

It surprised the world when the Argentine Cardinal Bergoglio announced that he would call himself Pope Francis I – a Jesuit taking on the mantle of a Franciscan, so to speak. But Francis of Assisi is a saint with universal appeal who, being an early environmentalist, is suited to our age. Where other saints might be seen as specifically Catholic – St Ignatius Loyola, say, or St Vincent de Paul – Francis has an ecumenical allure even to those who do not usually have much truck with sainthood. Margaret Thatcher, raised a Methodist, in a tradition where devotion to saints had little or no part, famously quoted the prayer attributed to St Francis of Assisi when she was first elevated to prime minister, outside Downing Street. Whether St Francis (who died in 1226) wrote the prayer is doubtful, but it is a very nice aspiration which begins:

> Lord, make me an instrument of Your peace. Where there is hatred, let me sow love; where there is injury, pardon; where there is doubt, faith; where there is despair, hope; where there is darkness, light; where there is sadness, joy.

Had she been more schooled in the lives of the saints, Mrs Thatcher might have realised that Francis was an unlikely match for a politician with a strong eye for financial good housekeeping. Francis himself was, basically, an early hippy who quit his affluent and, reportedly, frivolous life as a rich merchant's son to go off and embrace 'Lady Poverty' and live in a cave, addressing wild animals (according to legend) as 'Brother Wolf' and the lunar planet as 'Sister Moon'.

His affinity with nature led him to be named, in 1979, the patron saint of ecologists, but in his own lifetime he was within an ace of being excommunicated by the official Church for the nature-loving, which was seen as dangerously close to pantheistic paganism. Wiser – or perhaps shrewder – counsel prevailed and he was eventually authorised by the pope to start a brotherhood of roving preachers, who became the Franciscans.

It often happens that individuals who are at the margins of orthodoxy become, in time, the most successful examplars of the mainstream.

Again, according to legend, Francis started the tradition of the Christmas crib, which became the focus of the Christmas story for many centuries. When Pope Benedict XVI declared – with a somewhat literal attachment to Germanic scholarship – that there is no evidence that the ox and the ass were present with baby Jesus in the stable, he disappointed millions of children, some of whom had added pigs and hens. I'm sure St Francis would have approved, however, of the extra pets.

'Any life viewed from the inside is a series of defeats.'

George Orwell

The Archaic Elegance of the Necktie

18 October

The tie is probably on its way out as a marker of masculine style. I don't suppose that International Necktie Day is much of a cause for general jubilation.

Leaders of men often spurn the necktie these days: the late Steve Jobs, Alex Tsipras and Richard Branson are noted anti-tie icons. Mr Branson feels so hostile to the gentleman's necktie that he boasts of arming himself with a scissors, the better to go around cutting off ties.

Ties have seemed doomed since the big global corporations like Amazon, Google and Microsoft have favoured casual attire, and 'dress-down Friday' has migrated to the rest of the week. Neckties seem stuffy to the cool and the hip, even if they are still expected on some formal occasions – weddings, funerals and for any gentleman who joins me for tea at my London club. Michael Palin was refused admittance for being tie-less.

Those who like the necktie claim that it is both neat and neutral. A man wearing a discreet tie is not drawing attention to himself: a man wearing a pink shirt with his chest hairs showing seems like someone looking for notice.

And a tie can say quite a lot, in its own way. There are eighty-five ways to knot a necktie (according to a guidebook on men's style, *The 85 Ways to Tie a Tie*), and each expresses a feeling and a mood, and sometimes a character. Men who tie a very tight little knot are said to be mean. The extroverts have a floppy, loose style.

I have no strong ideological feelings about the male necktie, except that it can add a dash of colour to a man's appearance and it can enhance the looks of a very plain man. David Beckham doesn't need a necktie to look beautiful, but I can think of many an ugly mug improved by an elegant tie.

The necktie is also a reminder that men once were dandies. The great Regency dandy Beau Brummell would take endless care over his morning cravat. Many would be rejected until the perfect tie was tied. Jeeves would understand.

In America, the bow tie once represented 'the Intellectual': Ivy League professors favoured them. So, of course, did band leaders.

The tie's pattern can signal so many messages. Guy Burgess, Communist, spy, promiscuous, gay and drunk, ended up in a dreary flat in Moscow. He gave up king and country, but he could never relinquish his Old Etonian tie.

Well, at least there may be International Necktie Day celebrations in Croatia, from where the cravat derives. It seems it's still worth celebrating in Zagreb.

A Week in an Old People's Home

My son joked to my niece, 'We've put Mum in an old folks' home!' Yes: recovering from a hip operation, in my early sixties, I was treated to a week in a convalescent home, which was also a care home for the elderly and frail.

The experience was an eye-opener.

The location was a green corner of Kent, and my room looked out on a rustic scene of fields, trees and country pathways. In the distance, a pastoral scene of sheep safely grazing could be glimpsed. In the morning, you could watch the silvery hoar frost rising from the brambles, and through the day, the lovely changing kaleidoscope of nature's moods. I had books, music, television, my laptop: all the comforts.

I can't fault the home for its well-ordered management. But, oh dear, I found the change of attitude towards me as a person anguishing.

Once you are in a retirement home, it seems that you are almost automatically patronised, treated like a slightly slow-witted child and addressed in simple words and terms of endearment. 'Are you *all right*, Mary?' 'There *you are, dear*, sit down here!' 'How are you, *my old darling*, today?' 'Are we happy, *lovey*?'

I recognised that the helpers were trying to be kind, and they did what they could for the old ladies. Running any kind of institution requires rules and regulations, set times for meals and a daily routine. But I came to dread the communal mealtimes because they were generally conducted in complete silence. The ladies hardly ever spoke, beyond the most banal and necessary exchanges. 'Here are your *pills*, Doris. Don't forget them, my love!'

The intellectual stimulus was zero – the books, DVDs and magazines on offer utterly undemanding. Spiritual comforts too were thin on the ground – chaplains didn't visit often.

Being old brings many aches and pains of body, and sometimes brings a decline, too, in memory and acuity. But the worst part of it, I concluded from my sojourn at Sunset Hall (as I called it), was the gradual loss of identity – of the unique sense of personhood – that can accompany old age.

On the very last day of my stay, one of the old ladies who had said so little began to speak to me over lunch. One of her sons was coming to visit her and this had stimulated her interest. I asked her about her early life. An amazing story emerged. She had been one of the women officers who had worked in the control room for the Royal Air Force during the Second World War, in radio contact with air traffic, moving strategic pieces around an operations map.

She described how, every morning, she would see the young pilots scramble into their aircrafts – knowing that perhaps a third of them would not return. She counted them out and counted them back. It was an absorbing story of a riveting life experience, and as Sheila talked I reflected that every old lady there probably had some equally extraordinary experience wrapped up in her brain, never to tell it now, because nobody spoke to them in anything but patronising banalities. And no one thought to ask.

Don't Get It Right – Get It Written

An editor I once worked for in the newspaper business used to counsel young reporters struggling with getting words down on paper (as it used to be): 'Don't get it right – get it written.' The coda was: 'You can get it right afterwards.' This is a helpful piece of advice for anyone who suffers from procrastination (as most people do, at some point) or writer's block (as many writers bewail). It can also be a kind of guide, making a little bit of progress when you feel too daunted by any project to make a lot of progress.

Sometimes, facing a project that seems too challenging, I think: 'I won't get it all done. But I'll get something done.'

One of my early memories was being taught to read by a cousin of my mother's who had come to lodge, a retired schoolteacher. I see myself standing there as Cousin Honoria held the child's book in front of me, pointing to each word. I would have been, perhaps, five years old and jigging up and down, keen to run off and play. 'Come on, Mary,' she said, in a schoolteacher way. 'Just another little biteen more. You can do more than you think.'

'Just another little bit, then,' I said. I read another line, and then I remember thinking, *Hey, yes, I* can *read!*

Everything is a little at a time. Every accomplishment is about breaking down the task into component pieces. At Alcoholics Anonymous, people are advised never to say they are quitting drinking for a week, a month or a year. It is always: 'Just for today.'

I heard another variant on this theme with the phrase, 'You can't swallow the whole elephant at once.'

As for counsel regarding 'don't get it right, get it written', the French intellectual Roland Barthes put it in a more gnomic way: 'One cannot write – one can only re-write.' It's the rewriting that is important, but when something is already written, even in the roughest, there then exists a text to work on.

Sometimes I sit down at the laptop worried about starting an article and I remember what Maeve Binchy said: 'The hardest bit of writing is switching on the computer.' Get something written. Then get down to work on the text.

What to Put on a Gravestone?

I am wrestling with the question of what to put on my husband's tombstone in the local cemetery. After his name and dates, and a symbolic cross indicating adherence to Christianity, there is then space for a quotation of some kind. One of his favourite authors was Dante, and the most famous quote from the text might be apt: '*Nel mezzo del cammin di nostra vita: mi ritrovai per una selva oscura ché la diritta via era smarrita*' (In the middle of the journey of our life, I found myself again in a dark wood, that the straight way was utterly lost). The other contender was from Matthew 6:28 of the New Testament (the 1611 translation, known as the King James Bible): 'Consider the lilies of the field, how they grow: they toil not, neither do they spin. And yet I say unto you that even Solomon in all his glory was not arrayed as one of these.' This is such a poetic and unmaterialistic passage and so appreciative of nature, which altogether suits Richard's character – a man so unmaterialistic he never, to my knowledge, opened a brown envelope or a business letter.

Unfortunately, both of these quotations proved to be too long to fit on the standard gravestone, as ordained by the local council, and neither the Bible nor Dante really should be edited so drastically that it loses tone. A snappier quote was called for. I thought of Horace Walpole's axiom: 'Life is a comedy to those who think, and a tragedy to those who feel' – partly because it would allude to his sense of humour, and it would give the casual cemetery visitor something to reflect on. Still, I dithered. A friend who had known Richard for long years, Julie Steeples, suggested a phrase he would often reiterate when presented with some news about the state of the world, or humanity: ''Twas ever thus.' Pithy, and slightly intriguing too.

Or should I just stick with the thought-provoking words from a favourite hymn: 'The day thou gavest, Lord, is ended'? He always said that the night must come when work is at an end ...

Parking Wars

Many have been the debates about the source of war and aggression, and I've had a small personal epiphany into how conflicts stir.

Over a Christmas period, an unknown motorist had been parking his or her vehicle in a spot I regard as 'my' parking space. It's not, legally, my space, but it's a T line outside my garage doors (which are never used). A T line is a request not to park in that space, but it's not legally enforceable, according to the parking wardens.

But it's my turf all the same! How dare the usurper take it!

That's what I started calling the offending vehicle whenever I saw it on that spot – the Usurper. And I could feel a sense of territorial outrage. I peered into the vehicle and saw it contained various accessories which struck me as being more female than male.

Any time I was away for the day, or the night, it seemed, when I returned, I saw the Usurper parked in 'my' place. It irked me quite unreasonably.

I talked to a friend about it – a mild-mannered grandmother of a kindly cast of mind. 'Have you considered bashing in the Usurper's wing mirror?' she suggested.

'Mm,' I said. 'How about superglue on the windscreen wipers?'

'Or you could always scratch the paintwork with a key!'

Obviously, of course, these weren't serious suggestions. We were letting off steam and being sardonic. No need to raise the spectre of an incipient threat of vandalism. It was a light-hearted allusion to the vengeful emotions that lurk within our deep unconscious.

I could request the Usurper not to park on 'my' territory, but they might retort that the request wasn't legally enforceable.

Instead, I just snuck my car onto the disputed spot, deliberately not moving it for days. It gave me satisfaction to think that each time the Usurper would seek that parking place, it would be taken. Ha-ha.

Then, I asked myself, 'How petty can you get? What does a parking space actually matter on the great scale of things? There are families living in refugee camps – I have visited them in the Lebanon – desperate to keep everything together, hoping against hope that their children can have an education and a future. And you're worked up about a *parking space*. Pathetic!'

Solzhenitsyn said that 'The line dividing good and evil cuts through the heart of every human being.' And in a small way, that can even be discerned through parking wars.

The Usurper disappeared for a while, and I thought how absurd I had been. And then, a month or so later, she reappeared and parked over a whole weekend outside my garage.

Coming home one Saturday afternoon, I felt the old wave of fury at seeing my turf invaded. 'Don't worry about it,' I told myself. 'It's a triviality.'

I think I've conquered the irrational rage. Almost, anyway.

The Absent Mind

The French have an engaging phrase alluding to a *trou de mémoire* – a memory hole, down which known facts just disappear. The Americans call it a 'senior moment'.

It's a mortifying occurrence that happens with age. It famously strikes with a blank about names. There's a neighbour I know perfectly well and chat to on a regular basis, and suddenly, out of the blue, his name was swallowed up in that memory hole. I could think of his surname. I could think of his wife's name. But I could not find his first name, which has just disappeared out of my consciousness. It's not only mortifying. It's troubling.

All my contemporaries fear 'losing their marbles'. Especially since it happens to the nicest, most intelligent people. I have a lovely friend in Dublin who began to experience the onset of dementia when she was barely seventy. She had been so bright, clever and funny – and also sunny-natured. As her mind began to lose its moorings, the focus she once had slipped away but the sunny nature remained. The wonderful love and devotion of her husband remained a factor in her life whatever altered states of mind prevailed, and she never seemed unhappy. But still, it is woefully distressing to see a mind and a personality afflicted by dementia, or Alzheimer's, and it's small wonder we all fear it.

I also had a close relation to whom this happened, and I remember looking into her eyes for what turned out to be the last time and realising that there was no comprehension whatsoever. I remember leaving the care home in tears: tears for the loss of a personality and for the passing of all things.

Sometimes it is said that our minds, today, are on overload because modern life has become so complicated: our minds are like a computer whose memory is full, and until we either install new software, or delete some of the old data, these *trous de memoire* will continue to swallow information we should be able to access. There is also a theory that the memory drawer for names is especially vulnerable to slamming shut within the brain synapses. But I still wish it wouldn't, and I've taken to writing down more names.

One recommended method of fishing lost names out of the memory hole is to go through the alphabet hoping each letter might prompt. And so, I started: A for Alfred, B for Brendan, C for Charlie, D for David ... finally, the name popped out of the plughole: I for Ian!

She Died at Auschwitz

Edith Stein was considered to be one of the most gifted philosophers of her age. Born in 1891, she became a teaching assistant to one of the major German philosophers, Edmund Husserl, the phenomenologist, and also worked with Martin Heidegger. She had been born into an observant Jewish family but was, as a teenager, an atheist. In 1917, she had a long debate with Husserl on the subject of empathy, which, Sarah Bakewell tells us, 'led her to look for connections and bonds between people in a shared exterior environment, not a withdrawn and solitary one'. It was the opposite concept that Sartre would give us, that 'hell is other people'. She parted company from Prof. Husserl and then struggled to find another post. She was blocked by the University of Gottingen because she was a woman. She decided not to apply for a job in Hamburg because of her Jewish background – the university had a quota on the number of Jews they employed. Then she read the autobiography of St Teresa of Ávila and had a conversion experience. She became a Catholic and then entered the Carmelite order of nuns. After reading Teresa of Ávila's book, Edith Stein stated: 'I said to myself – "this is the truth".'

When she entered the Carmelite convent, she took the name Teresa Benedicta of the Cross. 'Things were in God's plan which I had not planned at all,' she wrote. And yet what lay ahead of Sister Teresa Benedicta was a harsh fate. When the Nazis came to power, she was moved, for safety, from Cologne to Echt in the

Netherlands (where she completed her thesis on St John of the Cross). Edith's sister Rosa – by now also a Catholic – went with her.

But in 1940, the Third Reich occupied the Netherlands and in 1942 began deporting Jews to the death camps. The Carmelites tried to move the two sisters to Switzerland, but it proved impossible to get exit visas. The Nazi authorities began raiding Dutch monastic communities for anyone of Jewish origin, and in Echt they found Edith and Rosa. The sisters were taken, with others, first to Auschwitz and then to Birkenau, where they were murdered on 9 August 1942.

The remaining nuns tried to conserve all Edith's papers, and eventually they were gathered together, sometimes in scattered fragments, and lodged in the Husserl Archives. In the 1950s, Lucy Gelber pieced them together and saved them for posterity.

Edith Stein, as Sister Teresa Benedicta, was canonised in 1998 by Pope John Paul II. She was also placed in a pantheon of German heroes in the palace of Ludwig II, along with Frederick the Great, Goethe, Kant, Wagner and Sophie Scholl, a valiant young woman in Munich who protested against Nazi cruelty and was executed for her bravery.

Edith Stein is one of the six patron saints of Europe. And I'd like to think that her sister Rosa will always be remembered too.

Becoming a Better Person

The *New York Times*, crediting one Anya Strzemien, has published a fifteen-point plan for how to be a better person. These are the instructions, somewhat abridged and slightly paraphrased. Adapt and amend as fitting.

1. Wear comfortable underwear.
2. Drink coffee. It is a great source of antioxidants.
3. Stare into the eyes of someone you love for four minutes.
4. Don't ghost (don't disappear from someone's life without saying anything).
5. Be nice to babies.
6. Dress in a way that makes you feel powerful. 'If you feel good in your clothes, it affects you psychologically, somehow,' says Novak Djokovic.
7. If you divorce, play nice.
8. Toss the cigarettes.
9. Get a pet.
10. Take on a seemingly impossible task – like Eric Hites, the 'fat guy' who decided to cycle across America.
11. If you'd like to keep your marriage together, stick it out. The romantic writer Ada Calhoun says: 'Life is suffering – and yet.'
12. Put sex first in a (conjugal) relationship.
13. Make sure you are the boss of your electronic devices.

14. Relish the phrase 'I'm too old for this'. It's liberating.
15. Be generous to those who have helped you.

As they say in the exam questions, perhaps only ten to be attempted
…

Liberation from Corsets

George Bernard Shaw was a great Irish playwright who wrote some wonderful plays, and a few over-talky ones as well. He had some naïve big ideas – he seems to have been quite taken with Stalin's Soviet Union (when a politically planted Russian waitress told him that she had read all his works, he quite believed that she represented the ordinary socialist proletariat) – but some great small ideas. Two of his finest campaigning ideas were (1) the establishment of public toilets and (2) the popularising of 'rational dress'.

The benefits of public toilets are evident so hardly need to be rehearsed (although it is dismaying to read of the closure of these facilities, when councils realise they can flog them off as real estate).

But GBS's second crusade still deserves retrospective honouring. At the time of his prime – say, the 1880s (he lived from 1856 until 1950) – women were greatly burdened by complicated fashions and, most especially, by the tyranny of corsets and stays. Amelia Bloomer (died 1894) first established the Rational Dress Society to free women from this sumptuary oppression in 1881, supported by two other ladies of fortitude. The bicycle gave wings to the cause of rational dress, but it took many decades to succeed.

Even in my girlhood – the early 1960s – I recall the admonition from my elders on the virtue of a good corset, and we wore something called a 'roll-on': that is, an elasticated garment over our knickers which did something of a corseting job (pulled your tummy in) and suspended your stockings at the same time. The mini-skirt and the marketing of pantyhose put paid to all that.

Bernard Shaw supported the cause of rational dress from its inception: simple, loose garments which would be, above all, comfortable. Rational dress was expected to be accompanied by socialism, sandal-wearing, pacifism, feminism and vegetarianism, as well as the bicycle. Actually, it is probable that the greatest facilitator of truly rational dress – the cheap, easy, comfortable clothes we can wear today – is globalised capitalism, which, seeing a market for cheap and easy costume and spotting a range of manufacturing bases in emerging countries such as China, Bangladesh, Thailand and Brazil, duly paid budget wages to produce them. In its turn, this has produced different problems of global inequality, even exploitation, which GBS would surely criticise, but it has also achieved rational dress. We freely don our jeans and untrammelled underwear and loose tops, hampered by neither corset nor stays.

Rapunzel – The Other Side of the Story

My granddaughters reintroduced me to the fairy tale of Rapunzel – that's the story of the baby princess who was stolen away by a wicked witch and kept imprisoned in a tower until she was a young adult, her beautiful golden hair growing longer and longer. Rapunzel is eventually rescued by a prince and restored to her rightful parents, the king and queen, and the wicked witch, Mother Gothel, is condemned to be reduced to ashes for her evil deeds in depriving the rightful parents of their adored child.

But some of my sympathy was for the wicked witch, who must have had such an unbearable yearning for motherhood that she stole the baby in the first place and then used every stratagem possible to conceal her and retain her – although, it is true to say that Rapunzel's true parents had also longed for a child.

And when the case of Zephany Nurse, in South Africa, came to light, I thought again of the Rapunzel story. Zephany was taken from the Grote Schoor hospital in Cape Town when she was just two days old. The woman who kidnapped her raised her as her own child for nineteen years, thus depriving the girl of her rightful parents. A chance encounter with another schoolgirl who looked very like her unravelled the plot, and it was established, by DNA, that Zephany was indeed the kidnapped child, and the law ordered that she should be returned to her rightful parents. The woman who took her, and raised her, was sentenced to ten years in jail.

And as in the Rapunzel story, I felt some sympathy for the kidnapper. Again, what baby-hunger drove her to commit the crime of child abduction? And how she must have suffered through the years of raising Zephany, knowing there could be a knock on the door at any moment?

In the Rapunzel story, there is no indication that the princess developed any attachment to the wicked witch. But in the reports about Zephany Nurse, it was indicated that the girl did have a sense of bonding with the woman who had abducted her and had come to regard her as a mother.

There must be a penalty for abducting an infant: it's a grave crime. But many a woman will feel a compassion, too, for those who feel desperate enough to appropriate a baby.

Gratitude Letters

I have to remind myself, always, to write a thank-you letter after hospitality or a gift. I haven't always done it, I know. It used to be called a bread-and-butter letter, and the usual rule was that you were supposed to write it immediately. You came home from staying in a pal's house: you sat down and wrote the thank-you letter there and then. You received an exceptionally nice gift: the thank-you letter should be posted pronto. Putting it on the long finger – 'I'll do it tomorrow' – is hazardous. Then it becomes a chore. But it is the true sign of a well-brought-up person that they know how to write a thank-you letter.

But is it still the expected practice? A text message or an email may suffice (as with letters of condolence). With Christmas presents, where gifts are often exchanged, it would be pedantic to write letters for each and every one. And yet, older people are often hurt and annoyed when gifts sent to offspring, grandchildren, nieces, nephews and godchildren are met with silence. For the recipients of gifts, moreover, it's a sure way of not getting gifts in the future – or, anyway, of receiving lesser ones. Thank-you letters are polite, but they are also, probably, a Darwinian reflex of survival: if you thank people and are nice to them, they'll probably be kind to you again some time in the future.

The basic point is that people don't like being taken for granted. My late husband used to quote those bitter lines from *King Lear*

– as a general application about human nature: 'Sharper than a serpent's tooth is a thankless child.' I do occasionally think that I am under-thanked for some of my efforts towards others, but then I remember that perhaps I too was many a time guilty of just the same offence. I might have sat down and written my formal thank-you letters as bidden – sometimes, anyway – but did I ever really thank those who cared for me and were kind to me? Not enough, that's for sure.

Adoptive Mum Meets Birth Mum

I met a most impressive young woman called Karen Smyth, whose father had worked with my husband many years ago on the *New Statesman*. That's to say, the father was her adoptive father. Karen, who is a beautiful black woman in her forties, was adopted by Mark and Sheila back in the 1970s. They were an English white couple who thought they were unable to have their own biological babies. After a couple of years, they adopted a second daughter of mixed race – part African and part Asian. And then, as has been occasionally known to happen, quite out of the blue, they conceived a child of their own, who turned out to be another girl.

'I thought you couldn't get pregnant!' Karen remembers saying to her mum. 'Well, I am now!' replied her mother.

The explanation that is sometimes given for women becoming pregnant naturally after adopting a child is that the hormones are somehow switched on by the very act of nurturing a baby. Or maybe it's just about relaxing – that's another theory.

In any case, it all worked out just fine. Karen loved her mum and dad and showed me a happy picture on her mobile phone of her wedding day, standing in a dazzling wedding gown between her parents. Towards the end of their lives, she also cared for Sheila and Mark as they grew fragile.

In adulthood, Karen came to meet her biological mother, who is a gifted poet. She had become pregnant at the age of sixteen, and she just wasn't in a position to raise a child alone. Before Sheila died, the two mothers met. The biological mother said to the adoptive mother: 'Thank you for looking after my daughter.' And the adoptive mother said to the birth mother: 'Thank you for the gift of your daughter.' (Actually, Karen herself puts it more informally: 'Mum said to Mum … and Mum replied to Mum.')

I went away from meeting Karen, thinking: 'Human beings are wonderful.'

Good Anger, Bad Anger

It has been taught that anger is one of the seven deadly sins (pride, covetousness, lust, anger, gluttony, envy and sloth), but anger has been updated in our time. Expressing one's anger – letting it out, anyway – is said to be good and psychologically healthier than keeping it all bottled up. The noted psychologist Dorothy Rowe talks about the 'inevitability' of anger, and believes that people who say they have 'no anger' are in denial. Or perhaps they have successfully repressed it.

Marriages are now said to be improved where the couple has a good, healthy row every now and again. Don't repress it!

And anger can be a motivator – something that urges you on to accomplish something. Many a good cause has been served by a sense of sheer anger at an injustice or even a personal snub. When a person says, 'It makes my blood boil,' that can be a source of energy. Writers often draw upon anger: Emile Zola's most famous public text – 'J'accuse' – sprang from the anger he felt at the wrongful conviction and imprisonment of Captain Dreyfus; Josephine Butler pursued her campaign against the sexualisation and prostitution of twelve-year-old girls in Victorian England with compassion, but also with anger at the exploitation and injustice of all trafficking and slavery.

Perhaps anger only becomes toxic when it is wild, malicious and disproportionate: the road rage that leads to a fatal incident;

domestic rows that go well beyond the normal confrontations; fury that prompts verbal abuse via social media or electronic messaging.

The novelist Tim Lott has suggested that there is 'good anger and bad anger' – like bacteria in our system: we need the good bacteria and we must fight the bad bacteria. In childhood, he felt great anger at being 'treated as stupid because of my working-class status' – and the anger made him determined to 'prove them wrong'.

Sometimes an irrational anger just wells up inside you. As with a toddler's tantrum, it often arises from frustration. There's a time to let it rip, but there's a time, also, when good old bourgeois repression taps you neatly on the shoulder and prompts you to keep it all under wraps.

Cousinage

Some years ago, I sat next to a senior Lebanese banker at a London dinner party. I was rather in awe of such a lofty person and aware that I was somewhat on the ignorant side when it came to high finance. So I asked him about his day. 'Well,' he said, 'first thing in the morning I speak to my cousin at the Singapore bank. Then I speak to my cousin in the Frankfurt bank. Then I speak to my cousin in the Paris bank. And later in the day, I speak to my cousin in New York.'

'I see,' I said. 'Do you only do business with your cousins?'

'No.' He smiled. 'But – my cousins I can trust.'

Back in the 1960s, there was a fashionable movement to abolish, or at least demote in some way, the influence of the family. The psychiatrist David Cooper wrote an influential book called *The Death of the Family*; the psychiatrist R. D. Laing claimed that schizophrenia was caused by family repressiveness; and feminism denounced the family as an incorrigibly patriarchal institution which only existed to uphold male power and preserve property (an argument that Engels too had put forward).

I remember these ideas very well, and even remember how I applauded them.

Ah, but. It's hard to get rid of something so deeply embedded in human nature. It's even possible that, as society becomes more atomised, the family is the institution that – like the Lebanese banker – most people trust best.

God knows families are never perfect. I am glad to learn that Freud believed that there was no such thing as a 'normal' family (and considering the complicated and sometimes unedifying lives of some of Dr Freud's own descendants, he could say that again). Very bad things can happen in families: from paedophile crime to scapegoating of a family member. And family feuds are simply ghastly. Small wonder it's said that civil wars are the most bitter of all because they are essentially wars between families. The nation, the tribe, is also a family.

Yet for all its malfunctions, dysfunctions and homicidal crimes – the first suspect in a murder case is often the next of kin – the family never perishes. It always reconstitutes itself in a new generation. It is universal.

As for cousins, how right that Lebanese banker was. I cherish my cousins more with every passing year and echo his words: my cousins I can trust.

Winging It

We used to talk about this when, as young journalists, we'd be sent out on an assignment where we knew very little about the context of the story – nothing, actually. 'Winging it' came, probably, from an old wartime song, in which the words 'coming in on a wing and a prayer' occurred. There was not much power left to the pilot, so it was a matter of managing as best one could. Another version of 'winging it' was 'busking'.

Bad trip, though, 'winging it'. In most circumstances, preparation is everything. Whenever you possibly can prepare for an encounter, an event, an appointment, you always deal with it more confidently. If you're giving a public talk, prepare it. Yes, there are exceptionally gifted and fluent speakers who can rattle off something beguiling without notes, but it's usually the case that they have done this particular gig before and have perfected the method. For most of us, we must do our homework.

Ah, homework! Some teachers and educationalists are opposed to homework for schoolchildren now, claiming that it's not essential and children don't necessarily learn more from home study. I don't know enough about education theory to make a judgement: but I do know that, in life, 'prep' (another word for homework) always, always stands to you.

An ace reporter I knew in my rookie days in London used to spend time in the British Museum researching tropical trees and birds so that, should she be sent overseas on an assignment, she could write: 'The Queen stood under the bonga-bonga trees, whose yellow flower is deciduous.'

Prepare, prepare and then prepare again.

Recently, I was telephoned by a radio researcher who asked me to take part in a broadcast, following an article I had written. He then asked me to tell him what I had written in the article, as he hadn't had time to read it. That, I thought, was really winging it. What shocked me was that this young person wasn't even ashamed to admit that he hadn't done his homework. Eventually, you are repaid in your own coin, and often with another twist.

Meeting and Greeting

Whenever I run into someone I haven't seen for a while, and that someone is a senior citizen (or even when they are not), I usually say, 'Hello – it's Mary Kenny here' (or, if someone knows me under another identity, 'It's Mary West here'). This is the cue for the meeter to reply, 'But of course, Mary! I know it's yourself!' Well, I explain, sometimes I have different coloured specs, or occasionally no specs, or weird hats, or altered hair colour, and sometimes I've taken off a few pounds (or maybe put on a few), and thus I announce my identity.

However, this is not the whole truth. I do it really because I wish other people would do it to me. I run into people I know slightly and, I'm sorry, I can't always remember their names. I'm old and decrepit and my memory is full. But people are offended, frankly, if you say to them candidly – 'I'm awfully sorry, but I don't remember your name.' Every human being is, after all, the centre of his own, or her own, universe, and that they should be so unmemorable that others might forget their names is an insult to their self-worth. So you just smile nicely and exchange greetings and say it's lovely to see them, and isn't the weather grand (or dreadful), and – this is usually a safe guess – how is the family? You can't remember what the family entails – husbands? Wives? Partners? Singletons? – but it's usually not a faux pas, like forgetting their name. But it's not because they're forgettable: it's just the synapses of the old brain.

Sometimes I get the name afterwards – by the method enumerated of going through the alphabet – but sometimes I don't. That's why I go around telling people my name – just to try and spread the habit.

Cheerfulness Aide

There are several academic studies which have found that the best prescription for cheerfulness for those over fifty is – go to church.

One very large and thorough study involved almost ten thousand people, interviewed over a span of four years. It was carried out by the secularist London School of Economics and subsequently published in the *American Journal of Epidemiology,* so its findings are considered highly reliable and respectable – even if somewhat puzzling to some of the scientists who carried it out.

The outcome of the research was repeated and consistent: churchgoing combats ordinary depression. Churchgoing helps mental health. One of the leading academics involved in the research, Maurice Avendano, concluded that: 'The church appears to play a very important social role in keeping depression at bay and also as a coping mechanism during periods of illness in later life.'

Wrestling with sociological jargon, the report's authors were baffled as to why it was that churchgoing generally has an uplifting effect. What really stumped them was that other, secular activities, such as volunteering for charity work – which also involved social engagement – did not have the same impact at all. Indeed, many of those involved in voluntary activity were *more* stressed and worried.

Measuring whether people were depressed, had suicidal thoughts, problems with sleeping or other symptoms associated with mental health issues, Avendano et al. wondered if, perhaps, people who were cheerful by disposition were more likely to believe in God. Their report pondered about the value of 'participation' in church activities, the Christian churches' ability to impart 'belonging' or other sociological explanations for their findings.

Maybe participating in a regular act of worship is simply natural to men and women. Especially if there is some decent music or singing involved.

Mary Quant's Car

I love the fashion designer Mary Quant's definition of a car: 'a moving handbag'. That is, you can just chuck everything into it, get into gear and go. I certainly use my vehicle just as La Quant ordered, and it's usually a tremendous mess. And I'm not the only one, I'm glad to say. I get into cars which are replete with dog hairs and the marks of old wellies, in which bits of children's toys float and other detritus hovers. These are lived-in cars. Cars that are too tidy and too clean (I make an exception for chauffeur-driven limos, for it is a chauffeur's job to keep his working vehicle in order) strike me as somewhat soulless. I have a similarly careless attitude towards small scratches and bumps on my vehicle: as the Italians say, these are honourable battle scars.

The poet Derek Mahon tells an engaging story about the culture of clean motor cars. Derek came from a very clean, tidy, spick-and-span Protestant home in Belfast, and like all spirited teenagers he eventually rebelled against his parents' values. One day, in teenage challenging mode, he asked his father: 'What exactly is your objection to Roman Catholics, Dad?' His father reflected for some time and eventually replied: 'Well, look at the state they keep their cars in.'

In the sum of life's anguish and struggle, a messy car is hardly the worst sin known to man, or even the worst sin known to Catholics: Mr Mahon Senior surely picked on a very small character fault, *sub specie aeternitatis*. And he had to think for a while to even come up with a fault so trifling. So I wouldn't hold it against his memory.

All the same, when my car becomes particularly untidy and seriously in need of attention, I think to myself: 'What would Derek Mahon's da think of this?' And every now and then, I actually do a bit of a spring-cleaning blitz on it, emptying out the travelling handbag of its accumulated detritus, and for a time it becomes almost respectable enough to park with confidence on the Shankill Road.

'What's For You ...'

There's an endearing Irish saying: 'What's for you won't go by you'; and it's comforting when it means that if you are destined for some nice development – whether it be small, like a jolly invitation for the weekend, or big, like a wished-for pregnancy – it will happen.

But it can be a little discomforting if you think that it might be something unpleasant or negative. If there is some horrible mishap coming your way – if you will develop a disease you have always feared – 'what's for you won't go by you'. You can take it either way.

It's the Irish version of 'kismet', which is an acceptance of fate. And accepting fate can be a wise way of coping with the inevitable. The Eastern religions and philosophies which lean on the acceptance of fate are sometimes seen as a way of being serene with the inevitable. Where nature is fierce, or food is scarce, or life is hazardous, you will have more peace of mind submitting to the inevitable and consoling yourself with the notion that 'it is written'.

What's for you won't go by you.

I take an à la carte approach to this. I like 'what's for you won't go by you' in the positive sense. If there's something pleasant in the pipeline of time, well, if it's for me, it won't go by me. But if it's something unpleasant – thank you, I'll struggle against it as best I can. I'd rather not choose the passive, Zen-like approach: I'll affirm my entitlement to step in and override the forces of kismet.

Maternity

Alice Meynell (1847–1922)

One wept whose only child was dead,
New-born, ten years ago,
'Weep not; he is in bliss,' they said
She answered, 'Even so,

'Ten years ago was born in pain
A child, not now forlorn.
But oh, ten years ago, in vain,
A mother, a mother was born.'

Alice Meynell (*née* Thompson) was a gifted poet, essayist and journalist who grew up partly in Italy. She married the writer Wilfred John Meynell and they raised seven children (one died in infancy) while living on the slender earnings of freelance journalists. Their London home attracted many artists and writers, and Alice inspired love and devotion in several poets, including Coventry Patmore, Francis Thompson and George Meredith. She was in the running to be appointed Poet Laureate in the 1890s, but perhaps the establishment wasn't ready for a woman. Alice Meynell converted to Catholicism – before her marriage she had had a hopeless love for her Jesuit instructor, Father Dignam; they separated voluntarily – and faith remained central to her life. Her sister was the equally gifted military painter Lady Butler, who died at Gormanstown, Co. Meath, in 1933.

Winter

Vitae Summa Brevis

Ernest Dowson (1867–1900)

They are not long, the weeping and the laughter,
Love and desire and hate:
I think they have no portion in us after
We pass the gate.

They are not long, the days of wine and roses:
Out of a misty dream
Our path emerges for a while, then closes
Within a dream.

Ernest Dowson was the epitome of the romantic, perhaps deca-
dent, wonderfully attractive and doomed Victorian poet, dying at
the age of thirty-two, afflicted by tuberculosis, poverty and drink.
His biography, by Jad Adams, is appropriately called *Madder
Music, Stronger Wine*, being a line from Dowson's famous poem
'Non sum qualis eram bonae sub regno Cynarae', from which the
phrase 'gone with the wind' is taken, as well as the words, later to
inspire a Cole Porter song, 'I have been faithful to thee … in my
fashion'.

'Vita Summa Brevis', a short poem of just fifty-three words, has
also been plundered for quotations. Dowson was much admired
by Yeats, by Oscar Wilde and by T. S. Eliot, both as a poet and
a very human person. Some critics have identified a theme of
paedophilia in his verse (he fell in love with an eleven-year-old

girl, although he didn't propose to her until she was fifteen), but Wilde wrote of Dowson, after his death in 1900 – 'Poor wounded wonderful fellow that he was, a tragic reproduction of all tragic poetry, like a symbol, or a scene. I hope bay leaves will be laid on his tomb and rue and myrtle too for he knew what love was.'

Dowson's childhood was sorrowful: his father died of TB, as did a sibling, and his mother killed herself by hanging. He had reason to be melancholy, but his verse is an intoxicating mixture of yearning, ruefulness and mysticism. Suffering can be productive of art.

Day of the Dead

If you want to hear the good news about human nature, just read the death notices in the local, or national, newspapers. Here you will read touching tributes to mothers, fathers, grandparents, aunts, uncles, nieces, nephews, cousins, children and friends who have been greatly beloved in their lifetime. 'Angela Mary … a wonderful grandmother.' 'Beloved husband, dad, grandad, friend and gentleman …' 'Beloved wife and much-loved mother …' 'Loving husband of sixty years, devoted father and grandfather …' 'Francis died peacefully … his beloved wife, children, grandchildren and the whole family will miss him greatly.'

Glimpses of courage and fortitude in the face of illness are seen. 'Annabel fought a long four-and-a-half-year battle with cancer and was determined that it would not stop her enjoying her life and her grandchildren.' 'Mary was a wonderful and special person and it was hugely comforting for us to realise the great number of people who felt the same way about her.'

A wide network of kinfolk is often included in the bereavement: 'Will be sadly missed by her loving husband, daughter, sons, sons-in-law, daughter-in-law, brothers, sisters, grandchildren, nephews, nieces [all named], relatives and friends.'

Thanks are expressed for the wonderful care extended by nurses, doctors, care homes and hospices. Church services and requiem Masses are arranged and charities named for those who have mourned the deceased ('A donation to Birdwatch Ireland has been made in everyone's honour'). Comforting lines of verse are cited: 'When you hear that distant call / Remember I am at peace'; and in the Irish papers, sometimes a line in Irish is added: '*I líonta Dé, go gcastar sinn.*'

We used to wonder, when young, why old people would read the death notices with such attention, but it is logical, since they are full of information. They are archives of sociology and family history – geography too, since they nearly always locate the deceased where they hailed from and where they flourished. They are also a *memento mori*: we will all (if our heirs and successors are minded to do so) appear in these columns.

They are by definition sad, and yet the milk of human kindness overflows at this well, and in that sense they are also mightily uplifting.

The Language of Colours

'What bright colours you're wearing!' exclaimed a voice behind me. 'You are a colourful lady!' It was a stranger walking her dog, and she was being perfectly kind and complimentary, I could see. People seem to think it is unusual when older women are decked out in strong colours. 'I'm just an old hippy!' I sometimes explain. Our town is like that – strangers address each other in quite a friendly manner (although no town on earth is as friendly as Manhattan, New York, where conversations are opened up entirely spontaneously. Take a bus in Manhattan and make friends – or at least acquaintances.)

I wear a lot of purples, coral red, apple green, azure blue (and my hair is mauve). With age, skin fades and I feel I need something to bring back some vivacity into my appearance. Beige can be a fatal colour for oldies, unless you are fearfully chic and beautifully coiffed, as well as being exquisitely slim – a slim blonde in great condition can look fabulous in khaki. But *chacun á son goût*, and, look, not everyone over sixty wants to look like an old hippy.

Colour theory is interesting. People go to colour consultants to be told what suits them best. Some is just common sense: a person with a red face should seldom wear a red outfit or they'll look like a tomato. A very pale person will look funereal all in black. It used to be said that 'blue and green should never be seen', but this is no longer regarded as gospel: it depends on the blues and the greens.

Sometimes green and green shouldn't be seen, since varieties of green clash. Some apparent mismatches can work very well – pink can match with orange, and the late Princess Diana wore purple with red very fetchingly.

Orange, coral and saffron are said to impart energy. I can believe it, too. Red, on a young woman, is sexy. Waitresses who wear red get bigger tips from male customers.

Women who need to ration their time limit their wardrobes to a restricted colour repertoire which always co-ordinates. I have a friend (and a family connection) who usually wears either red, white or black, and everything mixes and matches brilliantly.

Black is chic, red is dramatic and white is angelic, shimmering, translucent – on the right person. It's fabulous when someone looks bronzed from the sun. But I'm a paleface, and sometimes when I wear a white jacket that I like, I look like a trainee hospital doctor. White can be clinical.

I once wore a yellow jacket on a serious television programme – it was an edition of *Question Time* on BBC One. I worried the next day whether I had spoken sanely and articulately. A media friend, the broadcaster and novelist Roisin McAuley, phoned to say she'd seen the programme. 'Let me give you some advice, Mary,' she said. 'Never wear yellow.'

Seldom have I worn yellow ever since (unless it is harmonised with something else). But sometimes the colour of your apparel takes precedence over the content of your speech and that's why it may be important. A colour should express your personality, but not distract entirely from what you are trying to say!

The Coffee Revolution
(But Tea Still Holds Its Ground)

One of the most welcome social revolutions of my adult lifetime has been the spread of good coffee in Ireland and Britain. There were a few coffee houses in Dublin in my childhood years – there was always Bewley's and Roberts, but they were both in the centre of town and visiting meant a special occasion. The smell of coffee passing the front of Bewley's in Grafton Street was always a delicious aroma. But when people offered you 'coffee' it was usually instant coffee, and a decent cup of coffee was hard to find. After two years in Paris as a young woman, I was dismayed to find, both in London and Dublin, that a stimulating espresso or a delicious café grand crème was a rare treat. Today, thankfully, there are coffee shops everywhere, brewing and selling real, ground coffee, and being a professional barista is an honourable profession.

When, sometime in the 2000s, I sat by the River Lagan in Belfast one Sunday morning, drinking a faultless macchiato coffee (espresso with added hot water), I thought: *This is civilisation.*

Still, I'm glad that the Irish remain attached to tea and, according to Juanita Browne's delightful social history of Ireland's love affair with tea, the Irish are 'officially the biggest tea drinkers on the planet'. Many people in Ireland drink six or seven cups of tea a day. Tea is exalted by Irish builders who say it's incomparable on a building site; older people remember drinking tea while turf-cutting on the bog; and 'tae' has served every mood – a comforter in bad times and a cordial in celebratory times. 'Put the kettle on' is a metaphor for friendliness and hospitality. It's been well-observed that it tastes most particularly reviving and refreshing after childbirth – I remember that welcome cup of tea.

But just as the barista knows that coffee has to be correctly made, so a true tea-lover knows that a decent cup of tea requires a certain ceremony. Tea really should be made in a teapot – the teabag in a mug does not measure up for the true tea drinker. Most deplorable is the Continental European habit of offering a cup of hot water with a teabag on the side. That won't do at all. It's a regrettable fact that, despite globalisation and internationalism, Continental Europeans do not always know how to make tea.

The water must be boiling. The teapot should be scalded and rinsed. The teabag should be placed in the pot, and the boiling – re-boiled, if necessary – water should be added. Then the pot should sit for a moment or two while the tea settles.

Whether one adds milk (before or after pouring tea) or sugar is, surely, according to taste. The absolute purist will use loose tea-leaves rather than teabags, but as long as the teabags are of good quality, it seems to me that both are acceptable.

Children, these days, are seldom given tea. We drank it from the earliest years. Coffee and tea are both wonderful drinks, and for anyone who is quitting alcohol, they can be actual life-savers.

Politics Tests Friendship

Can people be friends even though they have very different politi
cal views? They can, providing they have another very strong
interest in common, and they either tacitly or explicitly agree not
to discuss politics. Say two people love the opera: one is a left-wing
socialist and the other a right-wing conservative (it has happened).
So long as they stick to deep discussions on Wagner and Verdi,
they'll be fine. Some terribly divisive political issue may, of course,
raise its head – in Ireland the referendum over same-sex marriage
brought out differences of opinion, while in Britain arguments
about Brexit became quite bitter – but friendship can survive if
underpinned by manners, affection and a sense of humour. And a
prudent decision to stay off a subject which brings disagreement.

In general, political differences tend to diminish with age,
because in old age you come to see that all these ideas and
debates will still continue just as before, long after you're
dead: so what's the point of letting them cause trouble now?
In Alcoholics Anonymous people are told: 'Identify with the
similarities, not the differences.' And that, I think, is wise.

But there will be fallings-out, and sometimes a political
difference goes a lot deeper than the political substance. As
Bertrand Russell once said, 'everything is really about something
else'. Two of the great French intellectuals of the twentieth
century, Jean-Paul Sartre and Albert Camus, had been good

friends but had a famous quarrel in 1951, which was ostensibly about the purpose of rebellion and revolution. Sartre was, at this time, increasingly favourable towards Communism while Camus was increasingly critical of the Marxist paradise: in his book *The Rebel*, he suggested there was no such thing as social or political perfection – even when a revolution changed everything, another revolution would be necessary to change everything once again. The argument was political, but it became personal, and hostile letters flew back and forth. They quarrelled and never really spoke again, and though Sartre had started the quarrel, he wrote kindly about Camus when he died in a car crash in 1960.

But was there an element, simply, of competition and rivalry to their quarrel, rather than the pure discourse over Marxism? And were Camus' cool looks, versus Sartre's frog-like appearance, an element in that rivalry? Under all quarrels, there is a subtext.

I differed from my late friend Mary Holland on many subjects, but we stayed friends just the same. Attending a summer Merriman School in Co. Clare, we even shared accommodation. One of Mary's left-wing friends took her aside and said: 'Aren't you concerned with your reputation – sharing a house with that Catholic conservative, Mary Kenny?' With loyalty and wit, Mary Holland retorted: 'And what about Mary Kenny's reputation – sharing living space with a liberal leftie like myself?' That's what I call friendship.

Waking the Feminists

Pom Boyd is an inspiring and experienced theatre director who supports women in the performing arts, and this is her Waking the Feminists personal manifesto to prompt creativity and still the voices of negativity.

- Honour the WTF voice inside you whenever you hear it.
- Never under-estimate the desire of the powers that be to silence a dissenting voice. Always look up the magician's sleeve and behind their back to see HOW the illusion is being made – unless it is actually a magic show, in which case go with the illusion.
- Men are not more creative, imaginative or gifted than women.
- Listen to the inner artistic director curating your work and censoring your output – ask yourself what gender it is.
- Don't be afraid of the awkwardness of truth, but don't be awkward for the sake of it.
- Breathing in is as important as breathing out: it doesn't matter how you create – outside in or inside out.
- Go to your biggest secret, your overwhelming shame, and you will find the wellspring of your creativity: it's up to you how you use it.
- Creativity is limitless: everyone can be creative, but not everyone chooses to live by their creativity.

- Choosing to make your living from your creativity does not make you special but you will have a special life.
- Differentiate between your creativity (arts practice) and your career: they are not the same thing.
- When collaborating with an artistic entity or organisation, be clear who is collaborating with whom, what is being given, what is being taken and who gains from it.
- Gender imbalance is an imbalance: it's going to topple eventually. In the meantime, push it!
- Anger can be useful but creativity comes from below the fire. Passion will bring you so far, after that it's cold, clear self-belief.
- Women are not better behaved or nicer people than men. Nor are they always supportive of other women.
- Solidarity with yourself is the first step, solidarity with other women is the second step.
- Solidarity includes being generous, being kind, being supportive. It does not mean switching off your critical faculties.
- In the face of your work being rejected, feel it and move on. If the rejection is born from injustice or inequality, be obstinate and make a stand.

Love Is Not All You Need

It's funny, but I don't really like that Beatles' song 'All You Need Is Love'. The tune is immensely catchy, but the message is really deceptive. You need a lot more than love to get you through this life – you need courage, fortitude, discipline and a sense of purpose. You need *resilience*. Love is wonderful, and probably even essential to flourishing, but the idea that 'all' you need is love can be harmful and misleading. Our parents and grandparents used to worry about children being spoiled by over-indulgence – in short, by too much mollycoddling love: they feared that love would be a ruination.

Yeats knew that love was not bestowed equally nor accessed easily. 'Love is not had as a gift, but love is earned / By those who are not entirely beautiful.' That is, by those who know they have to make an effort.

The most depressing movie I have ever seen (aside from films about the Holocaust) is the 1995 picture *Leaving Las Vegas*, billed as an 'erotic romantic drama'. The eroticism is mostly pretty dark, as is the storyline: it's about an alcoholic Hollywood screenwriter, Ben (played by Nicolas Cage), who checks into a hotel in Las Vegas resolved to drink himself to death.

He gets involved with a sympathetic prostitute, Sera (Elisabeth Shue), who herself has had a hard life, but she is moved by his despair and resolves to try and save his life. They do find a fellowship together, and indeed a kind of love, but all the love in the world cannot halt Ben's determined self-destruction, and the narrative moves relentlessly on as he indeed drinks himself into final oblivion. The original autobiographical novel was written by John O'Brien who subsequently killed himself. It's desperately sad.

'Love is all you need' is a message I often hear from the pulpit. I sit in the pew and think, love is a superb value, but it is not always enough. No amount of love can save an individual who chooses to be self-destructive. Love that is not reciprocated leads to a deadening depression. Although sometimes tough love has shown us a path. We do need love, but love alone can't always overcome all woes.

Some Conjugations

I am a gourmet.
You are a gourmand.
He's a greedy-guts.

I am diplomatic.
You are economical with the truth.
He's a bloody liar.

I am environmentally responsible.
You are environmentally aware.
She's a climate-change looney.

I am a patriot.
You are a nationalist.
He is a xenophobe.

I am truthful.
You are candid.
She is the soul of tactlessness.

I am business-like.
You are brisk.
He has a very bad personal manner.

I am a lively conversationalist.
You're extremely loquacious.
She'd talk the hind legs off a donkey.

I am neat.
You are organised.
He is anally retentive.

I am sensitive.
You are chippy.
She is neurotic.

I am a decisive driver.
You are a little reckless.
He's a danger on the road.

I am a sexually liberated person.
You are somewhat promiscuous.
She's a roaring nymphomaniac.

I am creative.
You are unusual.
He is weird.

I aspire to the best standards.
You keep up with the Joneses.
She's an egregious snob.

I am spiritual.
You are religious.
He's a right-wing fundamentalist.

My child is spirited.
Your child is naughty.
Her child is totally out of control.

I am a thinking socialist.
You're a trendy leftie.
He's a hypocritical poseur.

I am Renoiresque.
You are Rubensesque.
She's shockingly obese.

The Condolence Letter

I have to write a condolence letter almost every other weekend these days. ('Never send to know for whom the bell tolls; it tolls for thee.')

When someone dies, a condolence letter is a duty, though it is one that I have sometimes neglected. I have intended to send one, and then the time passed and I did not. There was uncertainty about an address, perhaps, and I didn't bestir myself to find the correct one. I now feel bad about this, and since the purpose of guilt, in my judgement, is to help one to review and revise one's attitudes and behaviour, I repeatedly resolve not to neglect letters of sympathy in the future.

And what to say in a condolence letter? I have come to the conclusion that it doesn't really matter what you say, in detail, so long as you offer your sincere condolences for the bereavement. If you knew the person who died – which in most cases you will have – you recall the good memories. If you didn't – and the bereaved person is your friend – then you concentrate on the person's loss.

Some people now send sympathy cards and the card manufacturers have developed a nice line in these. Miss Etiquette might still say that a letter remains the correct form, but sympathy cards can be tasteful and thoughtful and some people like to display them around the house, like Christmas greetings.

What would Miss Etiquette say about receiving condolences by email or text message? I think she would say it is better than nothing. Phone calls never go amiss, but they are not remembered as well as the written word. A friend said to me that the great thing about a letter is that you can revisit it later and read it again, and it is more comforting than ever.

For believers, prayers (and Masses) are always welcome. Atheists and secularists may not wish to be offered any spiritual comfort, so naturally you have to respect their wishes. And in grief, nobody wants to be irked.

By far the hardest condolence letter to write is when a young person has taken their own life. But the hardest letter may well be the most necessary. All you can offer is your sympathy and your presence.

In the normal course of sending a condolence letter – that will usually be a natural death in old age – a difficulty may arise if you didn't particularly like the departed person. You must then decide whether to exercise Christian charity and say something bland for the sake of the bereaved, or not say anything at all. It's not a good time to write and say you thought the departed was a pain in the neck and you're glad you'll never have to look at him over the water-cooler again. Nor is it a good time to confess to a bereaved wife that you once had a wild fling with her late husband.

Perhaps I have sometimes failed to write a letter of condolence from funk, from procrastination or because, deep down, I didn't really like the dear departed and didn't quite know what to say. But usually it's procrastination.

Yet a letter (or message) of condolence is always appreciated, so, when possible, it is always worth trying to do properly. When my husband died, I received such touching letters from old friends and acquaintances that it recalled Colette's words: 'I've had such a wonderful life. I wish I'd known it at the time.' Indeed, he had a wonderful life and I wish he'd known it at the time.

I also noticed an absence of condolence messages from some quarters. But I'm sure they too had their reasons.

The Greatest Restorative

I am not much of an admirer of the words of Arianna Huffington – she who launched the highly successful online publication the Huffington Post – because, though an immensely rich woman, she founded a publication with a policy of not paying contributors, including professional writers.

I don't object to online publications run on a shoestring which do not have the funds to pay those who offer work and ideas. But I am opposed to rich people who decide to go into publishing by exploiting those who provide them with the material for their product. Ironically, in America, the Huffington Post would be described as being on the 'liberal left', completely inverting what 'left-wing' historically meant, which was, essentially, about supporting the working class. Those of us who work for a living are the working class.

As it says in the New Testament: 'The labourer is worthy of his hire.'

One of Ms Huffington's crusades is to restore the value of sleep to our world. This, I admit, is a very good idea. It's daft that a lack of sleep has been promoted as something terrific. Margaret Thatcher needed only four or five hours of sleep a night? That's not admirable – it's a recipe for bad temper, ill judgements and brain fade.

But if the Huffington sleep crusade is an excellent idea, it is also a very old idea. Rest was the great Victorian panacea for all ills. Florence Nightingale was said to rule England from her bed, where she remained for the last forty years of her life, to everyone's approval. Churchill, being a Victorian, was very fond of his bed and would rest there for much of the morning (admittedly, he'd have been up late the night before, putting away a great deal of champagne and brandy). Darwin, too, was a man for bed-rest.

My uncle P.J., who was a doctor, born in the early years of the twentieth century, advocated bed-rest as a healing therapy. Early sleep was the great restorative. 'One hour before midnight is worth two after midnight.' Sleep and bed-rest are important to our health and well-being, and we need to take these seriously. Take it from the Victorians, if not from Ms Huffington.

The Habit of Habit

Over a celebratory dinner, old friends pressed me to have a glass of Prosecco, the Italian sparkling wine that is now often preferred to champagne. From my recollection it was a pleasant and refreshing drink. Alcohol hadn't passed my lips for some years, and I have generally been firm in saying, 'No – I don't drink.' But this time, I replied, 'All right – I'll have half a glass.' And so it was poured.

There is a belief that anyone who has shown the symptoms of alcoholism mustn't taste alcohol ever again, because the very taste 'opens the gate' to addiction. For some, perhaps even for most, this may be true, but human beings are infinitely variable in their composition, and reactions to anything are as variable as individuals.

Beware of generalisations. One size does not fit all.

I raised the Prosecco to my lips and took a sip. Then another. Presently, I took a third. I set it down and took no more. I might as well have been drinking water – actually, I would prefer to drink water. Give me a fresh, cold, sometimes sparkling glass of water any day.

The sparkling wine tasted, to me, of nothing at all, only something with a faint acidic note. I have completely lost the desire to drink alcohol – I, who once would feel insecure if there weren't three extra gin-and-tonics lined up at the bar for me.

One generalisation may be true: human beings are creatures of habit. You get into a habit of doing something; and then you get out of the habit. When you're out of the habit of drinking alcohol, it just fades away from your life. The *idea* of it can still summon up something inviting: champagne itself always seems so appealing as a concept (as does beer – even for those who don't like beer, its amber and thirst-quenching aspects seem alluring). But once the habit is gone, the experience can be meaningless.

It's when you are in the process of quitting the habit of alcohol that you need to be abstemious. And that process may take twenty years. But once the habit is gone – for me – it's gone. And no regrets for its vanishing.

An Answer to Hypochondria

All my life I've been a terminal hypochondriac. I remember thinking at the age of about four that I was going to die from some kind of breathing difficulty that very day. That should have been a warning to me – both the infantile hypochondriasis and the breathing anxieties – but in very many respects, I'm a slow learner, and it's taken me a lifetime to pick up on some of the hints that the Almighty is sending me. Now, in old age, I really am breathless with a chronic obstructive lung disorder, and fears about dying at any moment have become much more plausible.

That's what they put on a hypochondriac's grave: 'You see? I told you I was ill!' A neurotic fear of illness eventually translates into a realistic grasp of facts.

There is a treatment for hypochondriasis, or at least a way of managing it: you open a file, either on your computer or in an actual notebook, called 'If Symptoms Persist'. And into this file, you write down all your anxieties about the symptoms that are worrying you, or, as with the true hypochondriac, scaring you half to death. I see, from revising my own ISP file, that ten years ago I was worried sick – literally – about a bad stomach. All kinds of foods caused nausea and sometimes bowel trouble. I recorded a general feeling of 'seediness, queasiness, rolling (or rippling, as it were) through intestines … A feeling of "bile" … A strangely acute sense of smell … A bad taste in mouth.' I marked myself out as a martyr to my digestion and, naturally, googled every kind of cancer. I'm a collector of cancer symptoms anyway: how distressing (and unforgettable) is that brief passage in *Ulysses* when James Joyce refers to the nauseous vomit his mother coughs up when dying of liver cancer? And I've never forgotten the episode when my sons were at primary school and one of the fathers of the other kids had a bout of vomiting after a foreign trip. Within three weeks he was dead from pancreatic cancer.

But the benefit of keeping an If Symptoms Persist diary is that (if you survive – no hypochondriac imagines they will) you can scroll back the months and years and see that, actually, ten years ago, you weren't dying. Though of course you may be now.

Another Grammar Lesson

'I die, or I am dying. Both are acceptable.' The last words of a born grammarian.

The Future is Bright – For Oldies

It is now predicted that most people will soon live into their nineties, and men will live as long as women. So what will the world look like when so many oldies predominate?

- There will be more places to *sit down*, as in the streets of Paris, where there are delightful benches for a pleasant rest (made of wood, so not too cold on the derrière). Even Dublin Airport, in its great skating-rink of an arrivals hall, will eventually provide *places to sit*.
- There will be a boom in cruise holidays to just about everywhere.
- Actors will once again be trained to *speak up*, project their voices and not to mumble 'naturalistically'. Oldies love going to the theatre but frequently complain that they *can't hear a thing*.
- Yes, hearing aids will improve to the point where they're not fiddlesome little pebbles in your ear which cost thousands and can be lost at the turn of a head.
- There will be more movies like *The Second Best Exotic Marigold Hotel* – suddenly film producers are realising that there is a big demographic of older people who go to the cinema.
- Evening events will start at 7 p.m. and end at 9.30 p.m., on the dot.
- People won't have to consult ancestry sites to look up their family tree – their great-grandmother will be alive and well and living just around the corner.

- The retirement age will be eighty-seven (a serious prediction).
- University campuses will be full of students doing degrees in their seventies.
- There will be a boom in incontinence pads, inevitably. Architects will finally get the point that, when it comes to toilets, you always need more space for female loos – which involve separate stalls – than male ones, which mostly involve urinals.
- There'll be more publications about gardening and fewer about sex (maybe).
- There will be much more choice of clothes and fashions for the old, as the market grasps the fact that not everyone is size ten and aged twenty-three.
- Water bills will reduce, as older people tend to think that a shower every three days is quite sufficient.
- The art of the obituary will greatly expand, as there's nothing oldies like better than reading these mini-biographies of their peers.
- There will be a boom in audiobooks – so relaxing as you sit in your driverless car of the future.
- There will be a revival in religious worship, as the old have always gone to church more – and, besides, their doctors will recommend it, since church-goers live longer, are healthier and are less lonely.
- There will be periodic outbreaks of pedantry, as oldies tut-tut at the poor use of grammar, recalling previously forgotten schooldays when you might be rapped across the knuckles for saying 'Me and Tommy' instead of 'Tommy and I'.
- There will, alas, be more people suffering from dementia and Alzheimer's; but there will also be more focus on overcoming

these illnesses and more medical attention given to finding a cure.

- There will be more TV programmes like *The Antiques Roadshow*, full of oldies raiding their attics for forgotten treasures that might be worth a few bob.
- Books in print will survive successfully, despite iPads and tablets, but many of them will be shorter (and in bigger typefaces), as old people already complain that many books are just too long and heavy to lift for old hands. The novella – short novel – has already made a comeback.
- The arts will be in good hands – concert halls, opera festivals, art galleries and literary events are often financially supported and kept going by those of mature years.
- More restaurants and shops will offer the joys of tranquillity to accompany eating and shopping, as opposed to noise.
- Everywhere you look, you'll see Fifty Shades of Grey – artificially dyed blonde, red, chestnut and purple.
- Oldies will have voting power and purchasing power and this may lead to a more conservative society, yet youth will be worshipped more than ever: what is plentiful is always reduced in value, and what is rarer is always enhanced. The old will have the numbers, but the beauty and vigour of youth will appear more precious than ever.

The Uses of Mindfulness

Mindfulness has been enjoying a great vogue, and there's surely no harm in it, for it instructs practitioners not to allow life to be dominated by smartphones, electronic messages or other multi-media 'overload', because too much electronic connection adds to the stress and general disharmony of living.

Mindfulness gurus say that you must let your telephone ring three times before you answer it. This gives you 'pause time' to compose yourself, to align your body position and to give your whole attention to the caller. That's the essence of mindfulness. Be present. Be *in* the present. Focus on what you're doing. Draw a deep breath, and be aware of your breathing. 'Wake up and smell the coffee.'

Mindfulness tells us that when you drink a cup of coffee, take the cup in both hands and savour its aroma, its heat, its flavour. Don't rush at your caffeine fix, but walk purposefully towards it, thinking about your feet as they walk. Pay attention to what you are doing and, at the same time, remember that everything is passing, and this moment is just one of the many instants which add up to eternity.

I especially like the mindfulness rule that, when you are having a business meeting, you should *turn off all mobile phones*. You cannot practise mindfulness – which means concentrating on what you're doing and who you're with – if your phone is going continuously. I still remember, with some ruefulness, having a breakfast meeting at the Shelbourne Hotel in Dublin which was repeatedly interrupted by a friend's mobile calls – which she took. Aargh! Mindfulness!

Some elements of the mindfulness movement are really a reiteration of the old principle of taking time to think and reflect. One mindfulness practice, for example, is to sit in a café and watch people go by: don't read, talk or do social media – just people-watch. My mother used to do that in the 1950s. Actually, she went to Paris to sit in the Café de la Paix near the Madeleine so as to people-watch: she'd have been interested to know that she was into mindfulness.

Some of the practices draw directly on conventional religious habits. 'Grace before meals' was a mindfulness practice. There's a lovely painting by the German naturalistic painter Fritz von Uhde which shows a family pausing to give thanks before they eat. And so mindfulness recommends that before you eat you sit quietly for a moment, express inwardly a sense of gratitude for your repast and think, mindfully, of those kind people in the agricultural sector who have produced your food. It's thoughtful and serene – and an interesting example of reinventing the wheel.

Mindfulness practitioners are often enjoined to look at flowers, trees and the whole experience of the natural world. Allow nature to teach you stillness. Don't take the earth's bounty for granted. Good counsel. When I travel on airplanes, I notice that most passengers don't give the earth and sea underneath them, with all its seasonal wonders, even a glance – it's just taken for granted. So, yes, we should be reminded to appreciate our wonderful habitat.

Some mindfulness draws on well-known folk mottoes. One practitioner, Orna Ross, has given us this philosophy of life:

'It's good to have an end in mind. But … what counts is how you travel.' That's just an interpretation of the traditional French saying *Mieux voyager qu'arriver* (It's better to travel than to arrive). Though perhaps some people enjoy arriving at a destination too …

Mindfulness can be helpful to anxious and fretting individuals: it teaches that obsessing, dwelling on the past or constantly worrying about the future eats away at life. Live each day. Experience every moment. We only have the now. And the movement has, obviously, arisen to meet the frantic busyness of modern life which can be so destructive of reflection and serenity.

Still there's a nice Jewish riff on mindfulness practices: 'Breathe in, breathe out. Breathe in, breathe out. Forget this and attaining enlightenment will be the least of your problems.' Sometimes, the most engaging part of any philosophy is humour.

The Perils of Tidying

My late uncle Jim Kelly was very interested in the life of Father John Sullivan SJ, who has recently been made a 'Blessed' by the Holy See. Uncle Jim had been taught by the priest at Clongowes Wood College in Co. Kildare in the 1920s and Father Sullivan was, by all accounts, a remarkable, inspiring and caring teacher in an era when teachers and tutors could be rigid and over-obsessed with discipline. Corporal punishment was out of the question.

Uncle Jim had to quit his university course because the family money ran out, and Father John wrote some warm, wise and encouraging letters to his ex-pupil, which my uncle cherished.

But alas! Uncle Jim was married to a good woman, Aunty Dorothy, with many housewifely virtues: but she was a fiend for tidying up. One day, while her husband was out, she entered his study and 'tidied up' his papers, throwing away, among other things, the precious letters from Father John Sullivan.

This provoked a marital rift that was never entirely healed – there were week-long silences, which are almost worse than violent rows – and I, a witness to all this, have retained a deep prejudice against tidying up ever since.

A most awful book – which was, regrettably, a bestseller – was written in recent years by one Marie Kondo on the art of tidying. She recommends chucking out everything, virtually. Ruthlessly. She describes books as just paper with words, rather than precious objects of memory and pleasure. Ms Kondo has disclosed that as a young woman she was actually hospitalised for an obsessive-compulsive fixation about tidiness and order.

Marital rows are often about something else (like all arguments), and there were perhaps tensions between my uncle and his wife anyway, although usually kept, to some degree, under wraps. They were not well-suited, intellectually: he would have made a fine professor of the classics, whereas she rather had contempt for people whose 'nose was always stuck in a book'. Yet at a deeper level – who knows? People choose one another out of emotional need.

His side of the family took Uncle Jim's part (naturally), and afterwards referred to the day that my aunt 'burned the saint's letters'.

Father John Sullivan had a saintly reputation already in his lifetime. He travelled around by bicycle and was much given to helping and visiting the poor. There is great devotion to him today in Co. Kildare, especially around the village of Clane. 'Take life in instalments, this day now,' is his spiritual counsel. 'At least let this be a good day. Be always beginning. Let the past go. Now let me do whatever I have power to do. The saints were always beginning. That is how they became saints.' Perhaps his advice about the lost letters would have been: get over it.

Fairy Tales Are True

It's hardly surprising that the story of Cinderella is often retold in different forms – this fairy tale is over a thousand years old – and has been told in 345 different versions throughout the world. The original is probably a Chinese story, written around 850 AD, in which the heroine is called Yeh-hsien.

Some feminists disapprove of the Cinderella story because they feel that little girls today shouldn't aspire to marrying a prince and 'living happily ever after'. But folklorists will say that Cinderella is about something much deeper. As a psychoanalyst treating disturbed children, Bruno Bettelheim claimed that stories like Cinderella can help a child 'find meaning in life'. The child can perceive good and evil through such stories and can understand, also, that evil has its attractions. Many 'evil' characters in fairy tales – women included – are powerful.

Cinderella, Bettelheim maintains, is essentially about overcoming life's obstacles and being loved for 'your true self'. The 'ugly sisters', or as sometimes represented, stepsisters, place great emphasis on what money can buy, on social rank and on embellishment, while Cinderella is in rags. But she achieves (with help) ultimate self-realisation, and she overcomes the difficulties placed in her path, partly through character.

Children need to understand that life will bring adversity, and there will be struggles facing every individual. Bettelheim even maintains that it is cruel *not* to read fairy tales to children – it is wrong to allow children to grow up thinking that everything is about pleasure, reward and comfort, as consumerist values tend to imply.

My favourite fairy tale as a child wasn't really a fairy tale at all, but the story of Dick Whittington, as portrayed in pantomime shows at Christmas. I understood very well that Dick Whittington was setting off on a journey, that he would encounter many setbacks and that his cat would be his helper and companion. (Fairy stories, too, often feature animal helpers.) There was always a bit in the panto when Dick was tempted to quit his ambitions – of getting to London and making his fortune – and we, as children in the audience, had to call out: 'Turn again, Whittington!' and will him to go on, to not give up. That idea of persistence in the face of adversity appealed to me enormously; though, I suppose, in a way you could say that it was, in essence, another version of Cinderella. And of course in the end Dick Whittington reaches his goal and becomes London's Lord Mayor – all celebrate!

The Turkish Carpet

I have in my possession a small, quite pretty Turkish rug which I acquired in Istanbul, without ever having the slightest desire to purchase a Turkish carpet. But I wandered into a carpet shop in an Istanbul shopping mall, and from that moment on, I was doomed to leave that shop with the carpet under my arm (price, via credit card, €250). Turkish rug salesmen are notorious for their ability to persuade, cajole, manipulate and eventually, it might even be said, lightly coerce a customer into a purchase.

This particular gentleman was a master of the salesman's art. He was brilliant. He spun me a spiel which almost transfixed me into a reverie: this, I told myself, must be counted as among the uses of enchantment. I knew perfectly well that I was being spun a yarn; I knew I was the object of a soft-soap hard sell; and I suspected that the salesman thought I was just another naïve or ditzy European shopper who could easily be parted from her cash. But I was beguiled, couldn't summon the resolve to resist and agreed to the purchase. I walked out of the shop, not particularly pleased with my rug, but deeply impressed by Mr Carpet's powers of persuasion.

The credit card is likely a key element of this episode. I probably wouldn't have handed over hard cash, which always seems so much more 'real' than a card whose bill will not drop on the doorstep for another month or so. But it was also a lesson on whether we always make a decision entirely of our own free will or whether time, chance, circumstance and strong personalities can railroad us into agreeing with something we don't particularly want.

Maybe manners, true or false, also play a part: you don't want to seem mean, or disobliging, or a curmudgeon. Especially when shopping in a country which is, overall, rather poorer than the country in which you live. But the rug always reminds me, just the same, that 'consent' isn't always that simple. We can be ambivalent about entering into all kinds of agreements. We can be coaxed, cajoled, flattered, persuaded, and generally railroaded into a decision we haven't really chosen.

It's All Maintenance

My late sister Ursula used to say 'everything in life is about maintenance' and that reflection returns to me every season.

The roof needs repairing? Maintenance. The bathroom needs a complete makeover? Maintenance. The paint is peeling on the back door? Maintenance.

Your toenails need attention; your hands could do with a manicure; throw in an eyebrow plucking, too. It's all maintenance.

Every trip to the hairdresser is about maintaining the barnet on your head in some kind of order: maybe colouring it to stave off the grey; trimming it to maintain a shape; styling and conditioning it to keep it presentable.

A man shaving each morning is practising a form of maintenance. Even a bearded man must clean and maintain his facial hair.

The universe obeys the Second Law of Thermodynamics: everything eventually wears down, wears out and stops. But careful maintenance slows down the inevitable decline.

Changing into winter clothes prompts thoughts of maintenance. The fashionable New York woman dry-cleans her clothes every week. Maintenance makes them last longer and in better condition.

The prudent gardener prunes and weeds the garden with attentive regularity. Without maintenance, a garden becomes a wilderness.

Houses, without maintenance, go to rack and ruin. Unchecked vehicles turn more quickly to rust. And older car needs more frequent NCTs/MOTs to be maintained.

You go to the doctor for body maintenance. She measures the wear and tear on blood and organs, and when the cholesterol level seems to be touching a ceiling, a preventative medication is prescribed. Your system needs more maintenance.

The ophthalmologist examines eyes and searches for signs of decline, for floaters or distortions or dryness caused by too much time staring at a screen. Drops are prescribed and warm compresses suggested: ocular maintenance.

Dentists explore your mouth to detect plaque and decay, and the wonders of modern dentistry can suggest not only fillings but also implants and caps and impressive whitening procedures. Pricey, but it's maintenance. Without such care, you'd be a toothless old crone or a gummy old geezer.

Religious people go in for spiritual maintenance. They may go to Confession, or attend retreats, so as to refresh and maintain the state of their souls and to beckon 'good karma' for inner maintenance.

Relationships have to be maintained. The marriage counsellors have forever advised couples to make time for one another and not let their love grow frayed through ill-maintenance.

Friendships must be maintained through thought, contact, meetings, greetings, gifts, anniversaries, birthdays, Christmas cards and, nowadays, email. 'A man, Sir, should keep his friendships in constant repair,' Dr Johnson told his companion Boswell.

Brains have to be maintained – if you want to conserve mental agility, you have to 'take your brain to the gym'. Crosswords and puzzles offer maintenance.

Language needs to be practised to be maintained. The French will tell you *'une langue, cela se perd'* – language declines unless used and maintained.

A rich man once told me that money needs constant maintenance. First you have to gather it; then you have to maintain it; then you have to control it and guard it.

Thankfully, few women today must learn to darn socks – a task of great tediousness to which young girls used to be subjected, with the aid of a wooden mushroom. Socks today are, I'm glad to say, thrown away when they develop holes. The disposable society has freed people from the many time-wasting tasks involved with the 'make do and mend' of old-time maintenance.

I threaded a needle the other day, to append a loose button on a jacket, and recalled my mother sewing regularly to maintain well-worn clothes. Even if she found sewing relaxing, it's a form of maintenance we can do without. Sewing too much can harm the eyes, so you're maintaining apparel at the expense of vision.

And yet, despite our freedom from the maintenance chores of old – when kitchen flagstones had to be scrubbed, grates cleared out, stair-rods brassed and silver regularly taken out and dosed and shone with Silvo – we have acquired so many more accessories to life which need to be maintained. When we enter a house, we look for sockets to charge up our mobile phones.

The more equipment you have, the more maintenance will be required. Insuring it, caring for it and storing all that stuff is also a form of maintenance. And consider the in-box in your email program: the system must be maintained by daily attention.

Those who Tweet and go to Facebook must update and maintain their electronic feeds to keep their involvement alive.

Hippies and hermits seek freedom from the responsibilities that go with maintaining every aspect of a material life. They disappear to deserts and mountain-tops and ashrams to forget such cares. You wouldn't blame them. But even they must occasionally cut their toenails and launder their underwear. Maintenance.

A Chance Decision

My grandmother Mary Conroy was a Connemara schoolteacher with high-minded aspirations who thought about becoming a nun. She was being courted by a fellow schoolteacher – this was around 1897 – and thus considered the option of marrying, rather than the convent. So she took herself off to Claddaduff church on the exquisite western fjord of Connemara, just a mile from Omey Island, to seek inspiration. The church was empty and she sat in the pews in a state of reflection. 'If someone comes in by the main door of the church, I'll get married. If someone comes in by the side door, I'll enter the convent,' she vowed. You might think she was a flighty person, but she was deeply serious, highly intelligent, with a dedication to the poet Byron (considered scandalous in the Victorian period) and a scholarly interest in Egyptology. But she decided to make the decision of her life on a moment of chance.

Within a few moments, someone came into the church by the main door, and that tilted her decision, it seems. She married and gave birth to seven children (though she never quit teaching throughout her years of maternity: it was her responsibility to find a supply teacher in her place – and pay the locum, too).

I visited that church, Our Lady Star of the Sea in Claddaduff, Connemara, recently, and it is still much as it was over a century ago. But when I asked the times of Sunday Mass I was informed that there is now no Sunday Mass, for there's a shortage of priests, which is something that would have been rare in Mary Conroy's lifetime.

But how our lives hang on chance! I wouldn't have existed, and all the wonderful characters I have known who were her descendants would not have come into life either, had she taken a different decision at that church. Michael Frayn once wrote that as we wouldn't have known if we didn't exist, it wouldn't have mattered: he called the notional person 'Ivan Couldavebin'. But once you know, retrospectively, that you did come into existence, then that makes all the difference.

Christmas

25 December

People are divided into Christmas people and non-Christmas people. A lot of folks I know are joyfully Christmassy. They love putting up the decorations and decking out the tree and arranging the lights and making everything nice for everyone. They are to be praised. They add to the happiness of others and the jolliness of the season.

I am not a Christmas person. Maybe it's because I am neither very domesticated nor very practical. All the stuff around Christmas just seems to me like *work*. And, pardon the Scrooge note, expense.

Scrooge, in fact, was rather misunderstood. He is held up as a symbol of meanness and mean-spiritedness, but what poor old Ebeneezer really disliked was 'humbug'. He didn't like everyone pretending to enjoy stuff they didn't really enjoy, and in a way, you could say that was entirely honest of him.

Nowadays, Scrooge would almost certainly favour Christmas, as he would perceive it as an opportunity to make money, with all that Christmas 'marketing' and frantic Christmas shopping. Christmas is a time to max out the credit card – for fear of being viewed as a tightwad old Scrooge.

My dear late friend Clare Boylan and I had a pact that we would not give each other gifts worth more than a fiver at Christmas. It was great fun because it was a spur to inventiveness and spotting unusual and amusing gifts at budget prices.

I actually like the religious side of Christmas: the story of the poor Jewish family seeking shelter and finding 'no room at the inn'. The carols are magical. The babe in the manger is an emblem of the wonder of birth and new life – nativity. I think it was quite mistaken of Pope Benedict to claim that there is no scholarly evidence of the ox and the ass being present with the group. There's folklore tradition – that's enough for me.

But for the rest, Christmas involves too much work. I have many memories of sweating over a hot stove cooking Christmas dinners, swearing like a sailor as I tried to co-ordinate all the courses. True, there were some happy family scenes and the memories of friends around a table are sweet – and, when you think about it, Christmas cards are a warm-hearted way of people remembering each other. Oh drat it, I always soften in the end and say, like Tiny Tim, 'Merry Christmas to One and All!'

The Doll's House

I saw it in the window of a local charity shop for some time before the desire to purchase it overcame me. It was more than €100, which seemed pricey for a childish fancy – but then a charity shop is a good cause, after all. I murmured the old Irish adage to myself: 'What's for you, won't go by you.' If it was still there after a few days, I'd go in and buy it. And so, on a particularly bleak Monday afternoon, I did.

A doll's house. A large mansion-type doll's house, with a sloping roof and darling bay windows. As I was in the process of buying it I felt the need to say to the man behind the counter, 'Strangely enough, it's not for a child – it's for myself.'

'You'd be surprised at the number of ladies of your age who buy dolls' houses for themselves,' he replied. 'After all,' he continued, oblivious of our current protocols against gender-stereotyping in toys, 'grown men play with train sets, don't they?'

And so it was loaded into the car and taken home, and I gazed at it in some delight for a few days. It was so big, a passer-by had to help bring it in by the side door. The house rooms – and its attic – were empty, so there'd be all the fun of furnishing it with dinky furniture and little figurines going about their dolls' business. Yes, a prize possession indeed.

Why the attraction for a doll's house in these senior years? It's not as though I'm a Mrs Good Housekeeping type – the furnishing and maintenance of a home is a chore, not a pleasure, to me. I never read anything about interior decorating. Ah, but where the irrational yearnings of later life break out – look to the childhood. What occurred in the childhood years that prompted the later object of desire?

Yes, I did have a doll's house as a child but I was made to give it away. I don't remember a whole lot about the childhood doll's house, except that it was pretty and I liked playing with it. But then, when I was about six, Aunty Kathleen came along and started to lobby me about the virtue of giving away this treasured possession to another little girl who was poor and had few toys. At first I resisted, but Aunty Kathleen was extremely persuasive and, gradually, she separated me from my doll's house and whisked it away for the poor little girl who had none.

My mother, who had no interest in childcare, bowed to her sister-in-law's greater focus and, in this, greater will. Or perhaps she agreed with the general proposition that it was good for my character to give things away and that the poor little girl needed the doll's house more than I did. And in the greater scheme of things, perhaps Aunty Kathleen was right. Perhaps it is good for a little person's character to be chivvied into giving away their toys and their possessions. We would think it a cruel thing to do to a child today (aunties nowadays would be expected to purchase a doll's house for the poorer child as well), but in those olden times of my early life, children were early introduced to the idea of self-denial, with a little coercion.

It's interesting how vividly I remember, not the doll's house itself, but the reluctance with which I was coaxed into parting with it. I remember the feeling of sadness. But I also remember the lesson that it imparted. Perhaps you should give away objects that you treasure to someone who has less. Perhaps you shouldn't be too attached to objects anyhow.

And perhaps, in the fullness of time, they will come back to you, or something very like them will. Thus do I have a doll's house of my very own to play with, once again. It's like T.S. Eliot writes in *Four Quartets*: 'And the end of our exploring / Will be to arrive where we started / And know the place for the first time.'

The Reputation Economy

We're told young people are becoming more prudent about what they put on social media. Maybe word has got around that 'reputation is everything', and a foolish appearance on social media may well be stacked against you in years to come when you apply for that very responsible job as CEO of some worthy corporation or charity.

But how I hated it when stuffy old parties warned us against 'losing our reputation', sometimes quoting Othello: 'Good name in man and woman ... is the immediate jewel of their souls.' How small-minded and backward when a bad reputation condemns individuals and their families – whole neighbourhoods have been damned for the negative reputation they have garnered.

But the reputation thing is back with us because of the Internet: Michael Fertik says so.

Fertik, formerly of Harvard Law School, is an American management guru and author of the book *The Reputation Economy*. His thesis is simple: everything that anyone has ever written on Facebook or LinkedIn, everything anyone has ever Tweeted or put on YouTube, can now be stored forever. And subsequently retrieved and served up as troves of future information.

When you go onto Facebook, Fertik reminds us, somebody, somewhere is likely to be monitoring you. Algorithms are being developed which will enable access to every communication you have ever transmitted electronically, so just assume that everything you message is being recorded.

Never, ever, he says, put any personal confessions onto social media. Never transmit some jokey anecdote about how wasted you were at the weekend, how you woke up in bed with some bearded stranger or had a bit of a lark putting powder up your nose. However hilarious you think it might strike your pals – just bear in mind how it will reflect on your CV when the 'reputation engines' regurgitate this information just when you've decided it's time to go into politics or maybe run for president.

The 'reputation engines' of the Internet are a little like the Recording Angel of legend: everything gets noted. So 'be smart about social media', he counsels. But don't make the mistake of withdrawing from Facebook or other sites – because that, too, could be grounds for suspicion. The trick is to curate your electronic reputation cannily. If there is some youthful folly you would rather not have brought to light, create a lot more narrative and 'noise' around it, or embellish the facts with a flood of positive information as a distraction ploy. The information is, after all, being gathered by a machine, so confuse the machine as much as possible.

Soon, everyone's profile will be available through a 'reputation search engine': whether they have ever defaulted on a debt, whether they have a track record in trashing hotel rooms or whether they are perennial no-shows at restaurant tables they have booked. Your dating score will be noted, as your credit rating already is.

Even more sinister, the 'reputation engines' will also associate you with good or bad friends. If you have louche pals who renege on their loans, or are known to be obese, this may leak into your reputation – the old adage borne out: 'Birds of a feather flock together.' If your friends are flaky, you too are likely to be, according to the algorithms.

But there's a positive side to this reputation economy. It has enabled successful enterprises like Airbnb, whereby people rent out their homes to perfect strangers knowing that they can track the strangers' reputations. If you get a good reputation as a guest, you will get many more offers, and maybe discounted prices; but a bad reputation will soon diminish your chances.

Very soon, people will be able to 'check their reputation balance', just like we can check our bank balance. We can observe our 'reputation balance' go up or down, according to the virtue of our conduct.

Maybe the reputation economy means the end of private life. Or maybe it's like going back to a nosey-parker village society – the Valley of the Squinting Windows – where the postmistress listened in to every phone call and the dates between a wedding and a birth were calculated with hawk-eyed detail. Yet if those restrictive village societies were narrow and controlling, they usually had less crime because there was so much neighbourhood surveillance going on. Could the reputation economy reduce crime nowadays? Could we track violent men, for example, to reduce domestic abuse, and indeed homicide?

There's always a good side to any development. But excuse me now while I go off and curate my digital footprint, just as Maestro Fertik orders.

New Year's Resolutions

1 January

I believe in New Year's resolutions, and I especially believe in them when they fail. I first gave up cigarettes on 1 January 1970, but I finally quit in about 1992. A perfect illumination of the drollery attributed to Groucho Marx: 'Giving up smoking is easy – I've done it thousands of times.'

Of course New Year's resolutions fail. Sometimes they fail again and again. But what does it matter? Each time you make a new start and a new resolve, and that helps to set goals and aspirations.

I don't scorn the self-help books that promise self-improvement. We should always be working on self-improvement. We are all of us our own project for constant maintenance and development.

It's regrettable, to be sure, that sometimes it takes an entire lifetime to reach the self-improvement you've hoped for, and it's vexatious that just as you've got the hang of life, and worked out what you should be doing with it, you get all the signals that your time will soon be up.

But, look, as they say in the movie business these days – it's all a journey. And you know what the French say about journeys: *mieux voyager qu'arriver* – better to travel than to arrive.

On a prosaic, but somewhat self-satisfied, note, one area in which I have self-improved over the last decade is keeping up with my taxes. I used to be one of those people who disposed of all brown envelopes from the revenue by shoving them in a file and procrastinating indefinitely about opening them. But, gradually, I've improved my attitude and started to tackle my tax affairs – a chaotic orchestration of bits of paper everywhere – as a January resolution. New Year's Day is now the signal for sitting down and organising my tax papers in a methodical manner, examining expenditure and income over the last financial year.

It is not unlike examining your conscience, as you have to give an account of what you did in that twelve months, how prudently or foolishly you stewarded your resources.

Tax papers bring their own aura of philosophy. As Philadelphia's Benjamin Franklin so immortally said: 'There are only two things certain in this life: death and taxes'?

The Mantra

Sitting, stuck, in a traffic jam, fretting about being late for an appointment, is a good opportunity to practise the serenity prayer. Everyone knows the serenity prayer: even atheists say it, leaving out the God bit – or, when feeling desperate, leaving it in. 'God grant me the serenity to accept the things I cannot change, courage to change the things I can, and wisdom to know the difference.' It's been adopted by Alcoholics Anonymous, and many's the time it has helped me through the day (and the night).

You can sit in the traffic jam, fuming and stressed, or you can repeat to yourself, over and over, 'Accept the things I cannot change'. *Accept the things I cannot change.* There are a lot of big things we have to accept that we can't change – age, death, loss, some serious or chronic illnesses – but, still, I find the moment of traffic congestion (say, a five-mile tailback on a motorway) the most apt time to practise this attitude.

'Acceptance' is something that appears in all world faiths, and some would say it is merely making a virtue out of a necessity, like the lady who told Dr Johnson that she 'accepted the universe' ('Madam, you'd better,' he wisely replied). In Western tradition, we think too much acceptance is passive, and we're right: if men and women had accepted everything there would have been no struggle to conquer disease or change or ameliorate so many conditions of life – think of how the abolitionists utterly refused to accept the status quo of slavery. We should change what we can change, when it strikes us as right to change. We should be affirmative and active and energetic about not always being reconciled to the status quo. We can often change ourselves, if we are minded to do so.

We cannot, usually, change other people. Maybe a great orator can exercise an influence now and again. Maybe a great work of art can open a mind to insight and enlightenment. Events and experience will have a bearing. But the usual rule is that we cannot change others, and seeking to control them seldom bears fruit.

There are times when struggling against the grain is pointless. You have to know when to be serene about acceptance. It was never a natural condition of life for me but, gradually, I think I've learned – by being stuck in enough traffic jams and coming to realise the pointlessness of fuming.

Written on the Body

In my senior years, I decided to acquire a tattoo. Or two. First, I got a sweet little shamrock on my upper arm. For a second tattoo, I wanted some form of writing on my arm – a nice little motto or adage.

I pondered over the story I was told of Beckett's advice to an actor who feared he was failing at what he was trying to do. 'No matter. Try again. Fail again. Fail better.' This might be an inspiring aide-memoire, and the full quote is even longer, beginning 'Ever tried. Ever failed. No matter. Try again …' But then my friend Marjorie said it was too 'downbeat' as a permanent marker, and that sowed doubts about its suitability.

There's another Beckett sentence that is even more downbeat which I like: 'You must go on. I can't go on. I'll go on.'

My late sister Ursula kept a commonplace book of quotations and I perused this for inspiration. I looked at some of the shorter phrases she liked, which might fit across my wrist: 'The only really valuable thing is intuition' – that comes from Einstein. Marcus Aurelius, a Stoic from the Roman world who coined many a fine phrase, advised: 'Think not so much of what thou hast not, as of what thou hast.' Niftier, and more grimly realistic, is a Samurai saying: 'Expect nothing; be prepared for anything.'

A tattoo is something you have to think about, reflect on and feel committed to. I know people have acquired a spontaneous tattoo when blotto in Ibiza, and perhaps there's a madcap recklessness about that which is almost admirable, but, on the whole, it's not to be recommended. When you are planning your tattoo, you must bear in mind that when you die this is what will be written on your body. So I had to choose a message I really, really meant.

I pondered over Søren Kierkegaard's wise axiom: 'Life has to be lived forward, but can only be understood backwards.' I like this saying so much – and I think it's so true – but is it too rueful to look at every day? How about Nietzsche's 'Live dangerously'? Perhaps I did too much of that in my salad days.

I finally found what I wanted to have inked on my person. When I saw it quoted recently I knew it was exactly right. It's a phrase from John Henry Newman that is so perceptive and so reassuring: 'To live is to change ...' I have yet to have the remainder of this quotation inscribed: 'and to be perfect is to have changed often.'

How Boxing Nearly Died

Was Muhammad Ali (born Cassius Clay) the greatest boxer of all time? He certainly thought so, and so did many of his admirers: at the time of his death in June 2016, he had a global fan club who worshipped him, as a champion pugilist and as a black man who did so much to enhance respect for his race.

And he certainly did that most effectively: his braggadocio was considered brilliant and entertaining, and his unique self-confidence surely provided uplift for those who watched and followed him.

Ali was not only an extraordinary boxer – his claim to being 'the greatest ever' was no empty boast – but it could also be said that he saved the entire sport of pugilism from being banned. Before Ali, boxing was moving into the shadows of growing disapproval; without Ali, it might even have met with the same fate as tobacco – prohibited and disdained as an unhealthy pursuit.

From the late 1950s onwards, pressure was on to halt boxing, increasingly viewed as violent, degrading and medically unsafe. Both Sweden and Norway banned professional boxing, and in Britain a campaigning member of parliament, the late Dr Edith Summerskill MP, worked tirelessly to have it outlawed. She wrote a book called *The Ignoble Art* and introduced two private members' bills in parliament to get it banned. She was supported by her daughter Shirley, also an MP, and by many in the medical profession, and many people believed that boxing would surely be prohibited.

And then Muhammad Ali hit the world stage and took possession of the pugilist's art. He also associated it most particularly with the triumph of the black man.

Were it not for Ali's dazzle, boxing probably would have gone on to be banned in the UK, Canada and Australia – possibly even the US, where health campaigners were also revving up the cause. But race trumped paternalism, and once Ali became a globalised celebrity, all talk of banning boxing faded away.

The Summerskills' campaigns did help to bring in safer rules around the sport, and Ali's subsequent trauma-induced Parkinson's was evidence that brain damage could indeed be a hazard. But Muhammad Ali undoubtedly saved boxing, not just by being great, but also by showing that its association with the triumph of the black man is too strong to be gainsaid.

Wishing Time Away

A very kind friend has lent me an apartment in Brittany for a holiday, and I've been hugely looking forward to it. It's nice to have something to anticipate, but still I hear my mother's warning at the back of my mind: 'Don't be wishing your life away.' When we'd be counting the days until the school holidays, or counting the days until Christmas, or Easter (when you had to abstain from all kinds of goodies during Lent), or anticipating any number of future events: 'Don't be wishing your life away.'

Alas, too often did I wish my life away: in pregnancy, counting the weeks instead of enjoying every single day of that miraculous experience. I counted the days until the end of my contract when I was changing jobs, instead of appreciating the positive aspects of a situation I was leaving. I marked off weeks on the calendar when I was following a diet, or waiting for someone I loved to return home.

I've also counted the days towards something I've dreaded. A speaking engagement I agreed to and afterwards regretted. Every year, I dislike the approach of Christmas, because I associate it with stress and expense.

But when your days are growing shorter, and the end of your life beckons, you wish, heartily, that you had those days back again, which you were once so anxious to get past.

Journey's Beginning

Before leaving home for a long trip, I try to remember to sit down for a moment and have a pause for reflection. This was a practice I first encountered with my late, very dear friend Miriam Doggart (subsequently Polunin). Her mother had been Jewish Russian and it was a Russian custom to sit together in contemplation for a short time before starting out – sometimes the custom is acted out in Chekov's plays, particularly *The Cherry Orchard*.

It's a lovely tradition. It helps you to collect your thoughts, to be calm, to reflect upon the place you are leaving and to consider the final destination of your journey. It may also strike us as a kind of metaphor for life – yes, we're all on a journey: we start out; we wend our way through the various staging posts of travel; we change; we arrive. But one day we will leave for the final departure, and all the familiar accoutrements of home will be left behind.

Miriam was a wonderful person who died in her fifties, the victim of an arsonist who deliberately set fire to her family home, where she was visiting for a weekend and caring for her elderly mother. In her last moments, she tried to save a pet cat from the torment of dying by fire. She didn't have the chance for that Russian moment of reflection at the end, so, whenever I am starting out on a journey, I try to dedicate that moment to her memory and the gift of friendship and generosity that she left behind.

How to Achieve the Fountain of Youth

I have a friend who is past seventy, and she looks as though she might still be in her forties. Her face, her figure, her *arms* (no bingo wings, no wrinkly bits around the elbow) are all those of a woman thirty years younger. How does she do it? Has she had work done on her lovely, fresh face ('work' being our euphemism, these days, for cosmetic surgery)? Entirely possible. I indulged in a spot of Botox myself a few years ago, and I sometimes think it's time to have another dose of it.

Is she lucky in her genes? Some people look young because their mothers and fathers also looked young. That's possible – even probable. Dame Joan Collins, who has gone on being commendably well-preserved into her eighties, has admitted to 'good genes' in the presentation of her looks.

Has my friend had an easy life? A hard life shows on the face and the figure. It has been remarked that the childless often look younger than those who have had children, the care and worry of which have added wrinkles and grey hairs. It has been remarked upon that nuns often looked younger than their years, perhaps for this reason (in addition to the healthy formula for long life: early to bed and early to rise.)

Some or all of these factors might have contributed to my friend's astonishingly youthful appearance. But I would wager that the biggest factor of all is the same factor involved in every achievement: the priority of commitment.

If you are committed to staying healthy and retaining your looks as long as possible, you make it a priority in your life. You watch your weight and exercise; you swim and go to the gym; you take plenty of rest; you attend the beauty parlour and the hairdresser regularly. You commit to it. You do whatever it takes to attain and maintain your goal.

Looking youthful requires the same motivation as writing a novel, running a marathon or getting your kids educated to the highest possible level. Commitment. Dedication. Resolve.

Living in the Past

I love living in the past. Some of my happiest hours were spent at a now-defunct newspaper library in the North London suburb of Colindale, where stacks and stacks of old newspapers were kept on file, both in hard copy and on microfilm. I remember the anticipatory feeling I had when I went through those portals. To spend a whole day in the past, scanning through those old newspapers throughout the twentieth century. I was stepping through the Narnia wardrobe and emerging in that past world.

Old newspapers are a terrific read, partly because, in retrospect, you understand so much more and you can see so much more clearly what is going wrong. You are wise after the event. You can also exercise what the historian E. P. Thompson has called 'the immense condescension towards the past'. All these innocent people in 1935, or 1948, or 1956, or 1964, didn't know all the clever things that we know. But wait! The people who come after us, fifty, seventy or a hundred years hence, will look at all our follies with exactly the same response.

Newspapers of yesteryear are hugely useful for the record; they will tell you exactly who was at an important funeral and print a thorough roll-call of names of everyone – for example, who embarked on the *Titanic* from Cobh (then Queenstown) in 1912. Reportage lasts. Comment and analysis is much more frail. Commentators' views are seldom enduring because they are not in possession of the perspective of time. Nothing is more outdated that what some controversialist said in 1965. As a commentator, I am acutely aware of that.

The past is less threatening because it is over; I think it was Carlyle who explained that this is why it makes us less anxious. The past, really, is the only tense that I truly understand.

The newspaper library at Colindale closed, but the newspapers themselves are accessible via the British Library at Euston (and in the National Library of Ireland, too). They have to be ordered in advance, and it's a little more complicated, but they are still there. It was just that the entire building, housing all those old newspapers, had a magical appeal to me, and I loved the experience of immersing myself in time past.

The Existential Loneliness of Old Age

I've always been a reasonably self-reliant and independent kind of person: doing anything on my own has never bothered me, from visiting the cinema or the theatre to travelling abroad solo. I am sociable, but there's a liberating freedom about doing something on your own. You can, literally, please yourself. You don't have to consult anyone else. You don't have to compromise with anyone else either, by tagging along, out of politeness' sake, with what they want to do rather than just following your own whims and fancies.

It is only in old age that I have begun to experience the sensations of loneliness. I think it's that feeling, essentially, that Thomas Moore captures so well in his poignant and affecting, if perhaps sometimes sentimental, poem 'The Light of Other Days': how in the 'stilly night', memory brings the light of other days around him. He recalls 'the smiles, the tears / of boyhood's years, / the words of love then spoken; / The eyes that shone, / now dimm'ed and gone, / the cheerful hearts now broken.'

The loneliness of old age is not about needing someone to go to the movies with or a companion for a coach trip to the Austrian Alps: it's a more existential loneliness, of remembering all those we have lost and how much we should have relished their love and companionship. You look around a landscape which once seemed to teem with people you knew, and many of whom you loved, and suddenly, it seems devoid and empty. Moore compares it to being a ghost revisiting a banqueting scene: 'I feel like one / Who treads alone / Some banquet-hall deserted, / Whose lights are fled, / Whose garlands dead, / And all but he departed.'

There are many nostrums to help us to avoid loneliness in old age. There are clubs to join and places to go. The enlightened Arts Council of Northern Ireland has found that arts involvement helps everyone alleviate loneliness, and there are many studies which show that churchgoing helps to sustain a sense of community and, literally, communion with others. All this is fine and dandy, and all measures to diminish loneliness should be embraced. But it's the sharing of memories, the closeness and intimacy of remembering times past, the interlocking nature of what Thomas Moore calls 'the friends so linked together' that we miss, and whose absence makes us feel so existentially alone.

'Ah sure, the auld days were best,' an old crone told an Irish writer, Lionel Fleming, recalling the 1930s. Could she have been recalling the Victorian era which, though there were improvements, were still grim in Ireland? No, not that. It was 'the light of other days'.

What Do People Pray For?

'Miraculous St Rita – protect our beloved J.J. felled by a heart attack – that he be returned to us.'

'Protect my children and all the family. Give us the strength to accept and overcome the illness of our two boys. Help us to give of our best.'

'St Rita: my prayers that my daughter Angela recovers and my daughter Sophie finds true happiness.'

'St Rita – help me to endure illness!'

'For Alexander – seriously ill.'

'For my friend Brigitte, seriously ill. Watch over my family, especially little Yvonne, fifteen days old and fragile.'

'Look after my family and in particular my ill son.'

'St Rita: save my daughter and my grandchildren. Give me health.'

I am always moved to read the prayer requests written in supplication before a special saint or shrine; and these were some of the messages for St Rita in a lovely old church in Brittany. There is a universality about the plight of common humanity to the requests. We all have our worries and our troubles, and people must find succour in placing them before the effigy of a favourite saint. (St Rita was a fourteenth-century Italian woman who seems to have endured much suffering with fortitude in her own life.)

Some messages express thanks for recovery or other blessings. 'Thank you St Rita for curing my husband of prostate cancer. Watch over my children and grandchildren. My prayers are always under your guidance.' 'Thanks!' (in German). 'Thank you St Rita – from Patrick.' 'Thank you for looking after my family.' 'Thank you, O Lord, for giving me the strength that I need to look after those I love.' And most poignantly: 'Thank you for giving me my life, my God. Thank you.'

People don't often seem to pray for money, except perhaps to express general anxiety about the wider aspects of survival. 'Deliver us from all our financial problems, health and work.' Prayers for the general state of the world are less frequent than personal concerns, though they do appear: 'St Rita: bestow reconciliation on us. Send us peace in Syria, Iraq, Yemen and Ukraine.' And: 'Put hope and peace in my heart broken by the violence that roams in the world.'

There are many prayers for guidance in life decisions: 'St Rita, please look after me and guide me in my decision and trust it may be the right one.' 'I sent the letter: Lord, let it be well received.' 'For Baby and for my projects – that they work out well.'

'Give me confidence to face the future.' 'Help my brother Charles in his studies.' Many an Irish mother's penny candle has been lit in this cause.

Those struggling with difficulties are always mentioned. 'For Jean-Michel, that he may be helped with his handicap.' 'Help L.D., in her struggle for happiness after all the misfortunes she has endured without complaint. Thank you for blessings.'

And what mother's heartbreak must lie behind this supplication: 'I place in your hands the sorrows of our family – the disappearance of a son without motive, who has been out of touch for a year.'

The themes of birth and death are ever with us. Many are the visitors who light a candle in remembrance of those they love. 'Father, Mother and my brother Daniel: Rest in Peace. I love you and I will never forget you.'

(In German) 'For my father, who died today.' A summer visitor must just have learned of a father's passing and went straight to light a candle and record a message.

'Rest in Peace, Jordan, watch over your brother. Phil and Christiane.' One brother died, one remains.

And there are prayers in hopes for a baby. 'For Daniel and Catherine – that their dream of becoming parents is realised.' 'Eternal love! Let us hope for the fruit of our love! Jean-Louis and Anne.' 'That our marriage be blessed with a child.'

Rationalists may scoff that a wife believes that it's St Rita who has cured her husband of prostate cancer, rather than the interventions of modern medicine. But if a prayer written down in a church book helps, comforts or relieves human sorrows, then let it be.

The Burden of War

The first action of a British prime minister on taking office is a very sombre one. He, or she, composes their 'Letters of Last Resort' to the four commanders of Britain's ballistic missile submarines about what to do in the event of a nuclear attack, if the government should be destroyed. Nobody knows what a prime minister writes in these missives, and when she or he leaves office, the letter is destroyed. While the contents are secret, research has suggested that the PM instructs the submarine commanders to undertake one of four courses of action: to retaliate with nuclear weapons; not to retaliate; to use their own judgement; or to place the submarines under an allied country's command – probably either Australia or the United States.

What a terrible quartet of letters to have to write, and how they must bear upon the incoming prime minister, the huge responsibility of deciding whether hundreds of thousands of people – perhaps millions – could be obliterated in a nuclear strike or retaliation.

How grateful most of us are to not even have to think about such a terrible eventuality.

And how terrible are the outcomes of any nuclear strike. On 9 August each year our local parish marks an annual remembrance for the victims of Hiroshima and Nagasaki, where the atom bomb was dropped in 1945 to end the war in the Pacific. Some, of course, survived, but with such terrible wounds of body and spirit – and even genetically transmitted disabilities – that many would not want to be a survivor of any nuclear strike.

Yet which political leader would dismantle the arsenal of nuclear weapons, which would leave them, in the words of a socialist politician, 'naked in the conference chamber'?

The 'just war' theories of St Thomas Aquinas date from the thirteenth century, but they remain quite sensible guidelines: that war should be for a just cause; that every other method of resolving the conflict should be exhausted; that non-combatants should be, wherever possible, spared from the fallout; and that there should be a good chance of winning.

But on the psychology of defence, I have also been influenced by Rudyard Kipling's warning in his ferocious poem, 'The Gods of the Copybook Headings'. This is the verse that warns against disarmament:

When the Cambrian measures were forming, They promised
    perpetual peace.
They swore, if we gave them our weapons, that the wars of
    the tribes would cease.
But when we disarmed They sold us and delivered us bound
    to our foe,
And the Gods of the Copybook Headings said: *'Stick to the
    Devil you know.'*

And any British prime minister probably does have to consider that as the Letters of Last Resort are mournfully composed. But what a consideration to have to bear in mind.

Wise Words

When I was a young woman, I wrote to the novelist Kate O'Brien, and she, then quite old, very kindly wrote back. One line she wrote that I have remembered since is this wise reflection on the experience of life: 'We didn't ask to be born: but if we had been consulted, how could we have refused?' Some of us – perhaps many of us – were born into uncertain circumstances, were not 'chosen' children and faced many hurdles in growing up. But which of us would have refused the marvellous, miraculous experience of living?

What I want on my own gravestone is a few lines from a print published by the Cuala Press some years ago, by an anonymous author:

Oh, and how good is life –
Good to be born, draw breath
The calm's good: and the strife.

The Rainbow

William Wordsworth (1770–1850)

My heart leaps up when I behold
A rainbow in the sky:
So was it when my life began,
So is it now I am a man,
So be it when I shall grow old
Or let me die!
The Child is father of the Man:
And I could wish my days to be
Bound each to each by natural piety.

In sixty-one words William Wordsworth captures the amazing joy that a rainbow imparts any time we see it in the sky. His love of nature infused his work, but there is also a philosophy of life and a *joie de vivre* here that is unforgettable. A rainbow in the sky always seems lucky – and hopeful – and whenever one appears I think of Wordsworth. What a legacy.

Acknowledgements

I have visited many of the themes in this book in my journalism, and I'd like to thank and acknowledge the *Irish Independent*, the *Irish Catholic*, the *Catholic Herald*, the *Oldie* and the *Telegraph* papers for those opportunities. My thoughts on the medicalisation of melancholy came from a longer essay broadcast on BBC Radio 4.

I thank Ginny Dougary of the *Times* for the source of her interview with Rebecca Miller, who spoke to Ginny about her brother with Down syndrome. Thanks to Pom Boyd for permission to reproduce her Waking the Feminists manifesto. My Facebook friend, whom I know of old, Shen Brandt, provided the witty list of 'paraprosdokians', and Sarah Bakewell's engaging *At the Existentialist Café*, given to me by my friend Tony Duff, was a source of enlightenment on the life of Edith Stein and thoughts on other philosophers. I thank my son Patrick West, who knows everything about Nietszche, for also introducing me to Schopenhauer and his unexpected Buddhism. The priest who delivered the best sermon I ever heard is Father Eamon Whelan, Dublin-born, Kent-dwelling.

My thanks to my agent Louise Greenberg, a pillar of knowledge and dependability, and at New Island, to Edwin Higel and Dan Bolger – I am fortunate indeed to be associated with such an admirable publishing house. Most especial gratitude and esteem to

Emma Dunne, a superb editor whose literate eye, organisational skills and patient good humour are unsurpassed. Thanks to Marjorie Wallace for hospitality and inspiration, to Maura Meaney for unfailing encouragement, and to Ed and Emma West, to Valerie and Trevor Grove and all the Crouch End family who have shown me what really matters in life. Any errors and general misjudgements are, in life as in letters, my own.

Mary Kenny
Deal and Dublin, 2016